Waiting For Another

o

Julia Macpherson

Please note, this book contains references to suicide and self harm, which some readers may find upsetting

All net profits from the sales of this book will be shared equally (33% each) with Mind, the mental health charity and The Compassionate Friends, supporting bereaved parents and their families.

Quote from Julia (age 6)
on the arrival of her long-awaited baby sister, Sarah
(the name she was allowed to choose herself):

"The nicest word I know is SISTER..."

So this book is for Sarah, Julia's sister, best friend and soulmate;

also for Mia and Ciara, who will never forget their favourite Auntie.

ISBN 9781090600851

Published by Cerasus Poetry
London N22 6LY

www.cerasuspoetry.com

Foreword by Coral Jane

Dear Julia,

I'll bet you never thought this would happen - your book, I mean. We talked about it sometimes, but I'm not sure how serious we were and anyway, we talked about lots of things; like how we would grow old together and maybe run riot in the same old people's home, both being natural-born rebels. It's hard to believe I'm still here and you're not. How does any mother get her head around that?

Anyway, back to the book: this book. You always said I was the only person who really appreciated your writing, though that wasn't strictly true. You must have only been about eleven when your English teacher {whose life you made a misery in class with your bad behaviour} told me at parents' evening that you were 'the most talented pupil he had ever taught'. I never forgot that.

I think, for you, writing was your 'escape' during a life that had little stability and was frequently interrupted by illness. Books were your passion, too and it was no surprise that your first job after graduation was with the feminist publishing house Virago. You introduced me to many feminist writers and also to the poets who inspired you - most notably Sylvia Plath and the War Poets, such as Wilfred Owen and Siegfried Sassoon.

Following your unexpected death, I was handed a large red folder containing years of writing - some typed, with different versions that had clearly been worked on, including a few we had worked on together; others were simply fragments, scribbles on backs of envelopes, diary notes, scruffy notebooks. So much to go through, to sort out, to shed tears over.

Thank you Julia, for the privilege of being your mother. And it *was* a privilege, despite all the painful times. Thank you also for sharing these words and your innermost thoughts with me, as I now share them with others.

This has truly been a labour of love, but here we are at last, still *Waiting For Another Velvet Morning*.

Your Mum, always

Contents

Stumbling Home Through Butterfly Dreams   **5**

A Child's Song   6
Christmas In A Different View   7
Dying Wish   8
It's A Lovely Day (Outside)   9
Seven   10
The Hospital Bed   11
The Only Child   12
The Protector   13
The War Poets   14
This Time   15

And The Beat Goes On   *16*

Forget Her Blood-Red Fairytale   **19**

A Rhyme For Daddy's Girl   20
Diary Of A Hypochondriac   21
Family Roots   23
Lost And Found   24
Mother Of Creation   25
Mother   26
My Father And I   27
Reunion   28
Whole   29
Light Box (for Mia)   30

The Fly, Psychobabble And All That   *33*

In Or Out Of The Feathered Enclosure   **39**

A Battered Life   40
A Civilised Method   41
All The Fun Of The Fair   42
And God Created Woman   43
Bored Game   44
Feather-Lite   45

Feminism Under Threat 46

Indecision 47

Milk Of Human Kindness 48

Mine's A Microgynon 49

My Hot Tip For World Cup '94 50

Mystique 51

Supermodel 52

The Sacrifice 53

The Fly, Psychobabble And Nirvana 54

The Ruby Desire I Keep For You 61

Valentine From Berlin 62

Alien 65

Another Day 66

Colours 67

Dave 69

Dead But Not Forgotten 70

Dreaming 71

Gone In A Heartbeat 72

Green 74

Monsoon 75

My Poems 76

Night Dragons 77

Red 78

Resurrection 79

Sunday 81

The Return 82

Twelve Years 83

My Days With An Opium Eater 84

The Yellow World Of Smoke And Curious Faces 85

A Chemical Reaction 86

As Usual 87

At The Ear Nose And Throat Hospital 88

Branwell Clinic 89

Cream Tea And Wasps 90
Dear Doctor 91
Elixir 92
Falling Asleep 93
Hunted 94
Infectious 95
Less Than Nothing 96
Self Analysis 97
September In Norfolk 99
Sick Room 100
The Good Lobe 101
Wild Woman Of Wonga 102

The Day I Dared To Wear Lipstick 103

This Is My Posthumous Prose 105

All The Dead Girls 106
Blasphemy 108
Dark Ages 109
Easing Of The Soul 110
Knitting Unravelling 111
One Armed Combat 113
Peanut Crunching At Plath's Table 114
Peter – In Memoriam 115
Posthumous Prose 116
Species Under Threat 117
The Missing Generation 118
To Dust 119
Xmas '93 120
Some Velvet Morning 121

Danny Boyle, Darkness & The 27 Club 123

Author's Profile 127

Acknowledgements 128

Stumbling Home Through Butterfly Dreams

A Child's Song

I look puzzled at the happy, smiling faces
I smile too
If they are happy, I shall be happy
That girl is pointing at me
Oh, she is pretty,
What lovely curly hair
And merry blue eyes
She is laughing
I will laugh too
That little boy -
He is pointing at me
He is so full of laughter
Now all the other children are laughing
This is great fun
I shall laugh too
Now the pretty girl is poking me with her finger
She is laughing so beautifully
Now the children are dancing round me
How happy they are
I am dancing too
Now they are shouting things
They sound so joyful
Mongol! Mongol! they shout
So I try to copy them
Mongol! shout the children
And laugh all the more
I like to make them happy
But who is that I can see?
A little girl sitting on the wall
Looking at me
She has tears running down her face
How stupid! I like the happy children
Who are so nice to me

(One of Julia's earliest poems - age about 11 –
when children with Down's Syndrome were still described as 'mongols')

Christmas In A Different View

Swept away by final shrouds,
sanity and cash,
Christmas's laugh echoes,
climbing up from dusty
Christmases long ago,
still sounding the same.

Trees shed pines,
but no-one sheds tears,
except for her.

No amount of restraining helps,
when she hears laughter
and the rustling
of psychedelic wrapping,
parting to reveal useless items.

She curses Father Christmas,
who appears
with an evil glint;
his seasonal chortles
heavy with hidden mockery.

She cries
and knows
he is a devil in disguise.

Dying Wish

Wading through
the slime of youth,
it seems years
since he has loved.

Now, he must hate,
because he forgot
to misspend his youth
and now he wishes

he had lost himself
in some strange desire,
as he mutters an oath,
but not her name.

And there are no tears,
when the light goes out
and his youth is
spent by someone else.

It's A Lovely Day (Outside)

I want – *oh, questions* -
you are wise, too wise.
I need and shudder
and hear his cries.

You love your child,
who soon goes away
and somebody says,
it's a lovely day -

Ticking of a clock
at some strange hour:
it stops so dead
I see myself cower.

The room is so small,
walls running wild;
something so sad
happens to a child.

An odd sound, a wail?
As they stitch away,
I cry with you -
it seems a cloudy day.

Seven

he left me too, awash with blood
ran before he stemmed the flood
seven - and the smallest it seems

stumbling home through butterfly dreams
uniform blue, with a funny hat
he was so stale, blemished and fat -

insistence on what? i could not grasp
frail child's mind shook in his clasp
my underwear labelled age six to eight

knickers in innocence, shocked at their fate
whispery, evil, clammy and cruel
i knew he was breaking some deadly rule

echoes, sweet echoes, of a little girl's screams
reverberate along with salty streams
i could not know, though others knew well

i could only choke on the lingering smell
kindly plod, my statement complete
roared as i described "him" petite -

suffer little girl-doll, my tears wet the bed
whilst he drank and laughed and
killed his guilt dead.

The Hospital Bed

I don't understand -
I am puzzled by this cot-cage.
At home, I had a grown-up bed
and was very pleased and proud
and had just learned to use the proper toilet.
I don't need plastic pots with duck's heads to grip.
Now, I cannot get up and someone is forcing
a steel potty underneath me.
I cannot, I will not, endure the humiliation
of being a baby again - I am too old.
I hear myself screaming with shame, but
a woman in uniform shouts and shouts at me -
She is not my mother, but here is my father, alone
and he has brought me jelly babies - hides them
underneath my pillow from the cross lady.
Then, he is gone and I am scared,
so I eat all the sweets...

The lady is screaming at me, telling me I am
bad, not like the other children,
because I am so greedy that I have been sick
all over my bed. I did not know this before,
but now I know that I am a bad, evil girl
and I know it must be true, as my mother
still hasn't come. Is it because she now knows
there is a darkness in my soul, like the pictures
I have seen of the devil in books? -
I am only three - will I be this terrible person
for ever and ever? I feel all over dirty and bad.
When will she come?
Why doesn't she come?

The Only Child

I wanted, all the time,
some little friend, but
it didn't seem forthcoming.

I felt confused.

You would sometimes cry,
then silence would fall -
I couldn't think why
I seemed so alone
and disliked all my toys.

Mummy never knew
that I bullied the boys
and pestered you often -

Had you finally heard...?
About time, as well.
God had eventually stirred.

The first time I saw her,
I thought she was mine.
I was still delinquent,
but everything was fine.

The Protector

I watched you leave,
broken and uneven,
still lovely
and I wondered
and waited,
immersed myself
in green eye-shadow
and tottered
on platform shoes,
until you returned,
strange and shaky,
in need of protection -
so I held you and
in my child's mind,
shielded you
from such sorrows
I could not comprehend,
until you became
my protector once more.

The War Poets

He went to war
with Rupert Brooke,
envisaged glory -
a hero's return
or sweet oblivion -
and that death's kiss
would be fulfilled.

But soon, he found
the stench of bodies
a sour welcome
and the lies perpetrated
sang bitter in his mind,
as did the taste of the swirling gas,
thick with screams
from the boy next door.

Yet still, no bullet
embraced his fear;
instead, he quivered,
wet his trousers
and returned home,
puzzled and shaking.

He went to war
with Rupert Brooke,
but came home
with Siegfried Sassoon.

This Time

this time
you'll survive
come through
with flying colours

this time
no more lies
from people
who saw nothing

this time
we are friends
not the enemy
in disguise

this time
if you need anything
I'm here

And The Beat Goes On

... so the alarm goes and i'd only just got to sleep as i had a shitty night everything going round and round and now i have to get dressed to see the doctor i never dress and when i do i can only wear two dresses because that's all that fits me now oh how i hate myself i must get going but i'll have a fag first then on the way to the doctor's i start thinking about the ip and how for me it's not so much kerouac though on the road is fantastic to read i've not read his poetry so for me it's about lennon how he wrote a beatles song though you knew it was john because of the line how he blew his mind out in a car that's how he was one of us brilliant but fucked and i want to run home to my laptop and write

but then i'm at the surgery i have a fag outside it's one of my rituals i notice i have yellow stains between my fingers tell myself i must hide them from the doctor then when i see her she asks me how i am i get my list out because last time she told me off when i forgot something i had to go back but tell her i'm prepared so i start with the painkillers how i couldn't stand being me and feel like i'm cracking up so she says she won't cut my valium for another two weeks have i exercised yet so i say i haven't because i've been feeling ill well she says that's what painkillers do i ask for some antihistamines which she tells me not to abuse like before i say okay it's only when she gives me some nicotine gum she asks if i'm still not smoking and i lie and remember too late about the fingers then i say thanks

but i am thinking about my old doctor who i used to have a real laugh with and you know he got me he understood me he knew me inside out but he had to go to new zealand because of the fucking cuts the bastards me and him always agreed on politics and then i have to get down to the chemist and i'm so scared i'm going to buy painkillers and i know i mustn't but the compulsion is making me so ill i quickly buy some chocolate and a copy of heat instead and now that's sorted i'm back to the ip

then i'm at the chemist and i tick the back of all my prescriptions though it's illegal and i'll probably be done but i can't afford to pay for about a 100 items and then i trudge back home and when by the time i'm back home my nose is streaming and my dress is sticking to me what's this sweating is it the meds or my age i'm sick of looking like a tomato then i take about 15 antihistamines because i'll feel really ill if i don't but the bloody builders are making such a racket and i can't stand the noise and my laptop's on the blink i have a john cleese moment and scream obscenities at it so i go back to bed and

try to read about the holocaust which is all i can do when i'm like this and it sounds really sick but it's the only thing i can concentrate on and somehow i think that i will finally be able to understand how it could have happened but i never do so then weirdly i'm into the chapter about the nazi euthanasia policies for the mentally ill and it's not new to me of course because at the mental health charity i had to comment on how terrible it was and of course it was and then it got even worse and that was just a practice run for what came after which is completely indefensible you really can't go there

but i still keep wondering why my parents had me when they knew mental illness was on both sides and there are days i wish i didn't exist my laptop still won't work so i can't write it doesn't give a shit about my obsessions and the banging goes on and then that baby wailing howling as usual doesn't the mother feel like suffocating it but that's obscene and i must be a nazi myself i am so vile but none of it will stop my head buzzes like a fridge i must write i must

but then my husband comes in of course i don't bother to tell him about john the noise the baby the nazis the computer or the ip because i can see he's knackered and can do without me wittering on so we eat and while we watch amy winehouse i wonder why her not me then it's bedtime and we read together even though i've moved on to treblinka but the ip is still there i say to my husband i've got bad abc ocd he tells me to calm down write it tomorrow if i must then i tell myself i don't need to write it anyway because someone has already written about depression it's much better than anything i could ever write so dutifully i swallow my valium

but the drugs don't work they only make you worse but the ip is still there and like a junky which is what i am after all i have to get this down i am shaking as i write i have no idea if it's any good everyone has tried the ip this week they are all in a different league to me mine is crap compared to them and i feel so apologetic and inferior i am so useless then i wonder why i loathe myself so much but that's a different story so

maybe i'll ask someone off the site who is obsessive too he gives really good advice though he is so full of ideas i always have to make changes and i wonder if he's secretly an editor but what the hell he can look at it anyway and now at least it's quiet and there's no banging and maybe the baby is even sleeping insomnia always makes you feel like you're the only person awake going over and over things but on abc there's loads of other insomniacs thank god so anyhow i bow to the inevitable

like a tongue probing away at a mouth ulcer and even now i've got most of this down it's the same old my brain is still swirling the thoughts won't go i suppose i'll eke out the remainder of the night with tea and fags i should try to sleep but can't the adrenaline rips and rages through me now my other half has caught me and told me to come to bed for god's sake but the nazis are still there they're always there did the vatican collude could should the allies do more i'm exhausted

then i'm back to john lennon and how he sings i'd give you everything i've got for a little peace of mind shit mum will ring in the morning to see how i am i love her but just when i may have finally dropped off she will shout please pick up i'm worried about you i don't blame her i'd be anxious too is this any good if i had a daughter like me will i catch an hour where i can stop this hellish merry-go round there really never is an end to anything is there.....

Forget Her Blood-Red Fairytale

A Rhyme For Daddy's Girl

(for Sarah)

hi ho silver lining
swing her to the trees
songs for little girl-child
on her daddy's knees

sing a song of pink and gold
she always seems to cry
will she change as she gets old?
he was heard to sigh

tell me a story, she said
and looked into his eyes
he did, until he knew she bled
and then he told her lies

she floats serenely, woman-child
but inside something burns
he thinks that she is woman wild
never to return

so there goes his princess
daddy's pink-white prize
isn't she a frightful mess?
flaunting breasts and thighs

the squall of cherry-song anew
his cold heart murmurs dear
forgets her blood-red fairytale
too late to shed a tear

Diary Of A Hypochondriac

I was a baby with boxing gloves of
bandages, fingers festering - but apparently
I still laughed all the time.

Still small, my gills gasped for air,
nights spent over pyrex bowls of steam,
but between attacks, I was happy.

This is a cot and I'm in a big bed at home,
proper toilets too - yet they give me a metal potty.
I howl, humiliated and the incision hurts.
The nurse tells me, ever so quietly, that I am
very bad indeed. My mother is not here to fight
my corner - why doesn't she come?
My father brings jelly babies, which I eat for comfort...
Fresh wrath pours from the nurse, as I vomit.
I'm glad to get back to my grown-up bed.

In the heat of the Summer, my legs suppurate,
anointed in grease and bandaged. I was the only girl
wearing trousers all Summer. It was a little frustrating.

The children at school covered their eyes and refused
to hold my hand - made vomiting noises when I was near.
My best friend was the instigator, but we made up eventually.

The kitten had gone - I had taken it to bed, despite
my wheezing, just the night before... its fur matted with tears.
My father brought me Cluedo, which distracted me for a while.

The nurses were nicer than last time, but I hated the blood
on my pillow. They never gave me ice-cream, though everyone
said they would, but my mother was there and I loved the games
she brought and I loved her.

A baby came home, it was love at first sight, though I wasn't
allowed too near and had to wear a handkerchief over my mouth.
When I was better, I gripped her fiercely, my small body
suffused with love... and germs.

She's crawling on hands and knees, I want her to get up - she can't,
so I try to make her well and pray to a God I am already doubtful exists.

The 'grown' woman lies with drip attached, periodically it
fills with blood, my blood. My mind roams over the possibilities.
I begin to feel a little unhinged and press the buzzer,
but nobody comes. It remains unanswered. Even now.
Still unanswered.

Family Roots

You can trace it in my family tree,
bark broken and crusty,
its dust under your fingernails,
many branches withered by madness,
leaves scattered, trodden underfoot,
sodden with alcoholic rain.

When I was a fresh young sapling,
my sap was rising, I was green;
perhaps it was the ice age,
or toxic fumes from this age,
but I have become brown and fragile.

Can I be planted anew?
My roots are clotted with fungi.
Is there a tree surgeon brave enough
to tackle this disease?

Lost And Found

Misplaced my filofax in the park
I only noticed when it got dark
Left some books in a bloody cab
My lipstick vanished - felt rather drab

Dropped some change when I called you
My fags strayed in some obscure loo
Went on the underground, misplaced my fare
And when I wept, a bloke dared to stare

My sister's disappeared out in the East
I'm hoping she's somewhere far out at least
Don't think I'm distressed, or looking for pity
It's just some wine left on intercity

Forgot your number - no, tore it to bits
Shredded it near where the driver sits
So I've lost you too - it's no big deal
Unlike her, you were never real.

Mother Of Creation

(For Mum on Mother's Day)

She will splotch colours onto canvas, any old how,
to create something of unworldly beauty.
This art shines in her hair, which is full of Autumnal hues of red and gold;
her green - brown eyes are lit with reflections
of her dramatic, dazzling creations.
The textures she feels with fingertips amass, layer upon layer,
into mountains, streams, vales.
Knobbly, hacked and rough, they
make you want to touch, explore,
discover what thoughts are swimming underneath.
Her seascapes are no ordinary landscapes,
but mean something to her at that moment in time.
She scours the shore for driftwood, with which she will
frame this extraordinary work. Sometimes, she gazes
at the horizon and I know she sees beyond the waves
to far off lands that quicken her blood, but
which she knows are somehow beyond her reach.
She sighs and her thoughts are brought back to the beach
as she examines shells, sifts through handfuls of pebbles, all perhaps
representing a different hurt. The salt of the sea is on her lips,
reminding her of all her unshed tears. She does not know
or believe that what she is doing is something that transcends
everyday life and transports you to another, more spiritual dimension.
This is my Mother's work.
And it is miraculous.

Mother

Feline body stretching out for Mediterranean sun -
you've always hated this country, haven't you? -
wanting other shores, other seas.
We imagined you living in a cubic house
on a hill, overlooking azure hues,
painting and writing,
cats gathered around,
laughing at others' misfortunes.

We milked them until they were cream.
Sometimes, tiny ginger kittenish,
purring with pleasure at cuddles;
sometimes, almost like a tom-cat,
fur raised, claws out,
always ready to defend your young.

Even when we are no longer young
and my sister has her own kittens,
you will be dying, you say.
But from somewhere, you pull on your
inner mother and are there
if we are ill or sick in mind.
Not judging, just advising,
tearing out scraps from
your own past to sweep our fears aside.

You have caused us endless anxieties.
We haven't slept for worrying,
as you do for us;
but you are always, faultlessly,
our mother.

My Father And I

Shuffling up Oxford Street in my glass cage,
from which I peered, eyes half-closed in terror,
I thought of my father,
crawling to the doctor on his hands and knees,

hunched round Brighton, clutching his
tartan shopping trolley.
He would have collapsed without it.
These things I know and remember.

They are events that can only happen
to someone like me,
down in the gutter with the winos and homeless
and schizophrenics he despises and fears.

I am the she who represents degradation.
He would like to put his hand out,
as I drown in this unholy slime,
but he is afraid to get his fingers wet.

Reunion

He kept me mother, away from you
I wanted your love - I think that you knew

Tiptoeing through minefields together
Huddled in storms, rejecting the weather

Whenever you left, I gasped, lacking air
Clutched you and hid, wrapped in soft hair

The bubble of mother-love burst every day
Mine stayed intact - I still went away

Still alive - my voice grew so faint
Drug-weakened baby, not something to paint

Nervously winding round telephone wire
Thinking that I had avoided the fire

Pale chubby hands, dotted with blood
Gave birth oblivious, I'd land in the mud

Mother to daughter - a child was in need,
Now growing strong, at your breasts I still feed

Whole

The baby boy that went missing
left a gap in you - huge like the sun.
Now another him has left a hole
and you clutch at your scattered selves.

You think you are just pieces, fractured -
and I know you wonder if your mind
is loose, careering in your empty house.

But to me, you are utterly complete;
complex but whole, real,
always the total mother.

Light Box (For Mia)

These days, I gaze
Into my light box,
pray to the she-haze-Goddess
of Mother Earth.
It's not natural.

As if my own inherited soil
isn't sticky enough
with pesticides. As if I'm
not already sucking
lemon soporifics.
This is no entertainment.
It doesn't make my
sap surge like your smile.

On and inside black and white images
of sullen fruit, my disease barks.
Familial rot of rubber rooms
rooted, shot and flowered here.

Leaves are inconceivable with
genetic daisy-chain links.
Craw paw cactus I carry
means it's dry as dust
between my trunks.
Eugenics, cynics:
here's your field day.

The surgeons lopped,
never saw. I swayed,
always about to topple.
Why isn't my casket
full of spring?
Can't someone illuminate?
I am dimming; my dialling
mechanism fails tonight, as
my womb starts another futile,
over-rigorous maroon pruning.

I am wilting, as a muddy
morning oozes in,

sipping claying coffee.
Is this some kind of execution, as
I glare at my own Pandora's package?

What sick-startling jokes
have tumbled out, tricking
even my therapist?
What mind-toys may creep,
wreaking a devastation
not seen since Ypres?

But finally, a beam retina rolls,
rebounding a budding.
You dear little sapling –
I sang to you the other day;
voice rising, softer than I had thought,
then cracking a little.

I watch you trying to tell me
things you probably already know.
I can hear your beautiful baby words
that fertilise us all.
A tiny tulip – you don't
seem to stigmatise me
in the way
I do myself.

Your puzzlement;
the funny frown, so sweet,
like your mother's
at your age.
How I loved her.
How I love you.

The answer isn't in this
square of blinking bulbs,
it's inside my own fuzzy-lush
enclosure. Mossy but
half-hidden orchids
are so exotic, hypnotic.

At last, I have connected.
Rays reflect as sunflower seeds grow.
I glow pink-cream-gleamy.
You too hold your own
Buttercup Sundays
in your tiny palm.

Welcome to our fresh-new dawn.

The Fly, Psychobabble And All That

To say I was apprehensive would be minimising how I felt that night. Already, a sense of terror had pervaded my thoughts. I now knew what the aristocrats in France must have experienced on their carts, hauling them off to the guillotine. The following morning, I was due to start at some new place, rather pretentiously labelled a 'psychotherapeutic community'. My Doctor's explanation was that it was all very innovative and the success rate was high. I harboured doubts about whether it would make a difference, but my mental health was so crap I would happily have devoured heaps of horse manure if someone had convinced me it would help.

Then it happened, completely eclipsing my previous fears. A tickling sensation arrived in my ear the same time as a buzzing noise. I closed my eyes and listened to what sounded like a dentist's drill reverberating through my pillow, volume increasing ominously. Instinct told me a fly had sidled into my ear, but fear for my sanity soon replaced initial thoughts.

I tried to rationalise this unforeseen event. Could insects actually crawl into a person's ear? Surely that was impossible. And yet, I began to actually think it had. I began to wonder if creepy-crawlies could possibly gnaw into a person's brain. Not knowing what else to do, I got up and looked at my medical guide. The reassuring tome, written by one of those TV Doctors, who generally have a shiny smile, neatly combed hair and home knitted jumpers, in order to appeal to middle aged women, was getting rather tattered. It fell open at a particularly worrying section, the contents of which created overwhelming panic every time I read it. Why read it then? Why do dogs sniff each other's bottoms? They can't desist, nor could I. It was the chapter on bowel problems. Do you have alternating diarrhoea and constipation? I do. Have you been under any stress? Don't ask stupid questions. Is there any blood? Actually, yes. Is the blood in the stool itself? Well, how do I know that? What colour was it? Even with the help of my torch, that was a tricky one. Is the blood on the lavatory paper? I thought it was. And so on.

The myriad permutations of symptoms went on for pages. I appeared to have them all. The summary of diagnoses included; irritable bowel syndrome, haemorrhoids, ulcerative colitis and cancer of the colon. During my numerous visits to my GP, clutching the dratted book, I tried to convince him that there was something horribly wrong with my innards. His refusal to investigate further, telling me I was merely experiencing a health panic, had led me to dread my bodily functions. When I tried to explain this new development to him, it became clear he thought I was teetering on the brink of madness. Hence, sending me to the psychotherapy centre. That night, I started to see where he was coming from.

But anyhow, that night, even the pages on bowel difficulties left me disinterested.

I frantically flicked through the pages. Astonishingly, considering the vast range of complaints the cheery Doctor described, there was nothing on insects secreting themselves in ears. Even under problems with ears, a sudden revving in one's ears was not covered. I threw the book across the room. I searched for my secret stash of valium, which I had hidden from myself in a vain attempt to stop myself taking any. They had been obtained from a very inebriated and unscrupulous pharmacist. I found them easily and took every pill, hoping I wouldn't wake up. I had visions of a pathologist doing the autopsy and being astounded to find some kind of insect lodged in my grey matter. Cause of death: unidentified animal in brain.

Naturally, I did wake up. And yes, the buzzing was still there. I checked the window, hoping that last night had been a terrible hallucination, to see whether a fly or wasp was loitering behind the curtains. But there was nothing. Just the insistent, nightmarish zzzzzing of something in my right ear. I was stuck in an upside down, acid induced version of the horror film `The Fly'.

Somehow, whether, I was imagining it, or whether the fly was real, I knew I had to get myself to Camberwell. To therapy. I knew I was very, very ill. For some reason, I put on a striped top that revealed a bit of my midriff and a quite short, cream skirt. Then I put on tons of make-up. It didn't occur to me that I looked like I was on the game. I had just felt, irrationally, that if I was going to be dragged off to some locked ward, I didn't want to look like a bag lady.

It was 10.00am on the dot. We all sat in a circle. There was about 12 of us. I was introduced to everyone and I tried to smile without showing the gap in my teeth and the terror in my kohl-circled eyes. Some people looked reasonably friendly. Some just ignored me. Then there was silence, punctuated by tobacco-induced catarrhal coughs and scrapings of shoes. The droning in my ear continued unabated. The invigilator Andrew asked how everyone was feeling. Silence. Except for the jumbo jet thing going on in my head. One woman was frenetically swinging one leg and yawning at very frequent intervals. She was about 50 or so and was also wearing a short skirt. Admittedly, she had good legs, but her face was criss-crossed with lines and her skin drooped like a bloodhound. I was probably going to age as quickly as that, if I continued to be tortured with the road drilling thing for the rest of my life. How long do insects live anyhow? Perhaps ad infinitum, if it was a giant one.

The woman continued with her leg wiggling and the yawning for about 25 minutes, until Andrew asked her if she had something on her mind she would like to share. She got up, muttering that everyone always picked on her and proceeded towards the exit. Andrew, rather half-heartedly, tried to stop her. I decided to take my mind off the lawn-mower roving around my head and asked her why she felt she couldn't stay, adding that it may help her. As though her salvation lay in this room, which, even at that early stage, I knew it didn't. At this point, everyone glared at me, except for one young man with startling aegean-azure-eyes, who winked at me. The woman replied that there was no point staying, *because everyone hated her. I wanted to avoid provoking more antipathy from everyone, so just shrugged. She slammed the door behind her. The silence continued until the end of my first session.*

I already knew where the smoking room was, having availed myself of this facility during my assessment. I headed straight for it. It was no bigger than a cupboard but it was still a good retreat from everyone. That is, until about 8 more people squeezed in. We simultaneously lit up, sucking in nicotine and the majority of the communal air. It was then that people started to articulate themselves. First on the agenda was Caroline, which was, I gathered, the name of the woman that abruptly left the room. Several people told me, not unkindly, that the best way to approach the problem that was Caroline, was to just leave her alone. Apparently, she was an appalling attention seeker. It was pointless to reason with her. That's the way she was and she wasn't going to change. I agreed to blank her from now on, not bothering to ask why Caroline was there if she couldn't, wouldn't, question her behaviour.

The boy with the blue eyes told me his name was Peter and asked me how I was feeling. I realised he was gay, which was rather a relief, because he was also very good looking and the last thing I needed was any extra complications. Whilst we were chatting, I experienced an illusion that the fly was zig-zagging frantically in order to get out of the outer canal of my ear. I felt a surge of optimism. Surreptitiously, I stretched my ear-hole as wide as possible, giving the thing an opportunity to free both of us. But to no avail. The zipping seemed to surge, as though the beast was frustrated. And I wasn't?

Involuntarily, I looked up at the window. I still had the faint hope that this was actually an external situation and I had just, overnight, developed extraordinary powers of hearing. I asked, in a quavery voice, whether anyone could see a fly, wasp or bee at the window. No-one said anything, just looked at me curiously. Peter told me not to worry, there was nothing there and asked sympathetically if I had a fear of flying insects. This triggered a long conversation with everyone happily delving into their weird and wonderful phobias. The subject matter would normally have been just the thing to pique my interest. But, at that moment in time, I could only wonder, yet again, whether I had finally lost my reason. I wanted to bang my head against the wall and either kill myself or the creature haunting my orifice.

But this was supposed to be the place where talking healed you, right? So I steadied my shredded nerves. I told everyone, too loudly and rapidly, exactly what I was pre-occupied with. You could have cut the silence with some fly spray. My confession had been a huge mistake. Then the whole room, ignoring my rather bizarre utterance, started again to vigorously discuss the objects or situations that triggered paralysing fear. Only Peter realised I really was suffering. He didn't seem to give a shit whether he was conversing with a madwoman or not. He told me *what I was experiencing was awful and offered me some valium. They were blue ones, extra strong. We companionably munched a few. Then he suggested that I see the `on-site' shrink. This hadn't occurred to me before. It was clearly the way forward. What a great place this was, after all. I would soon be sorted. I thanked him profusely for the advice and valium and told him I'd see him later.*

I knocked at the door. This was not the same psychiatrist that had assessed me. He told me, beaming, that his name was John. He asked who I was. When I told him my name, the bright look on his face palpably faded. He enquired warily what I wanted. I explained my predicament. He laughed heartily and informed me I had been watching too many episodes of Casualty. I replied that I never watched the programme due to my psychological condition and asked him what he meant. He told me in great detail, still chortling merrily away, about a fascinating episode, only shown the previous Saturday. Apparently, an elderly lady had arrived at casualty in a state of distress, complaining of a buzzing in her ear. She was promptly diagnosed as being psychotic, until some bright young spark thought to examine her ear and actually found a fly flapping about.

Heartened, I told him that's exactly what was happening to me. He assured me that was not what was happening to me at all. In my specific case, the noise was just a symptom of extreme anxiety. I asked him if a fly, or any type of insect, can eat into your brain and questioned him too, about the longevity of creepy, buzzy things. He refused to disclose any information, explaining that, if he did so, he would only temporarily reassure me. He would simply be feeding my health ruminations. He went as far as asking how I would cope should I, in reality, have some insect the size of a brontosaurus in my ear. I declined to answer and started to cry. I walked out, continuing to sob loudly. That sadistic sod had been my final hope.

I was unsure what step to take next. John had pushed me way too far. I knew, from reading about fear and obsessions, that he had tried the `flooding' technique. I also knew that it was an intolerably harsh approach so early on in my so called treatment. I sat in the grounds on a bench, chain smoking. Then I had what was probably the most lucid thought I had had all day. I walked out the gates and went to the nearest shopping centre. It was completely inadequate, but I spotted a bookshop. Thank God. I headed straight for the medical section. There were only three medical books. Shaking, I leafed through them. The last book was perfect for my specific requirements. Eureka.

Now I knew what approach was necessary, I headed home. With the true hypochondriac's desperate need for relief, or to know the worst, it had to be done. It was an essential step, regardless of the outcome. I avoided the centre. I didn't really care if anyone stopped me. It was all crap anyhow. I hated everyone there except Peter. Psychobabble bullshit.

At home, I got some olive oil and tried to pour it down my ear carefully, but some of it slopped out down my neck and dribbled down the inappropriate top. I ignored it. I was a woman with a mission. I blacked out images of the shrink shaking his head and reaching for the straightjacket. Satisfied that the affected ear was full of oil, I tipped my head towards the bowl I was holding under my ear. I looked into the bowl. Floating on top was a corpse. It was a fly. A really big bastard, too. I was euphoric. The incessant noise stopped immediately. I was not psychotic. Neurotic, anxious, obsessive; yes. Psychotic; no. Well, I didn't think so then....

In Or Out Of The Feathered Enclosure

A Battered Life

ascension in a striped balloon
her time had run out too soon
gold and red soared up alone
for her sin could she atone -

they found her in a diamond sky
asked her questions, made her cry
then she screamed, seemed to float
emitted a gurgle from her throat

justifiable self-defence?
tabloids saw through her 'pretence'
reality trembled, evading her now
could not remember their final row

perhaps a tender mind was worse
than the beatings or missing purse
spring unattached, to weep and rust
does brittle crack? surely it must -

endurance torn, she drifted away
clothes ripped and limbs in disarray
mumbling, unseeing, shrouded in white
killed her opponent, but lost the fight

A Civilised Method

A metal serpent inside me.
It's not the bait, I know,
but little does he think
of thousands of fleeting years
etched across the sand.
A camel, tried and tested;
they do the same to me.

Why is my inside fighting,
uterus flinching, pulsing?
My womb can hardly breathe
and in the dark, I dream,
as my fear starts to uncoil,
unravel with a wicked grip
and strangle a spring of life.

All The Fun Of The Fair

Show you a fuss of gorging gripe
Helter-skelter, my egg is ripe

Violet tensing, fingers cramping
Cuts of streaking, silent stamping

Toffee apple wrench, is it all mine?
Suck it with vigour, soon to feel fine

A clench of teeth, sweaty and sliding
My groin ablaze, organs colliding

Gold carousel, grinding on down
Bitter shades seeping, turning brown

My agony ugly, cracked and cold
Lost for amusement, am I too old?

Abdominal feast, starting to grow
I'm on a rocket, it won't let me go

An acidic gut, lurch and subside
It took me for a leg-clamping ride

Clanking music comes to a stop
Climb off the horse, waiting to drop

Strawberry ice, cycle complete
Trodden in mud, candy floss sweet.

Fairground familiar, oh can I stay?
Just for another twenty-eighth day

And God Created Woman

Right now, her best friend is her hot water bottle,
her abdomen seeks its furry caress,
but to refill it requires movement -
something she cannot envisage
without carving-knife pain -

Blood, sweat and tears have taken on a new meaning
as she seeps, floods - a living waterfall,
crying at the mystery of this part of her body
that is not visible - her mind roams around
the monstrosity, rioting in her pelvis.

Feverishly, she asks questions no-one can answer;
the only reply the doctors, the men she knows,
can give her is to tell her: she is a woman,
this is your lot; so she curses Mother Nature,
who is really Father Nature...

Bored Game

come on down, play the game
every month the bloody same

can you guess what's in the box?
Mrs Tampax - fortune knocks

while the wheel spins round and round
a winning shriek, but make no sound

have you heard the standing joke?
take B6 until you choke

can you guess the going price
for a week in paradise?

I could win a real fortune
for my egg without a spoon

climb a snake, avoid my ladder
while I swell, I'm getting sadder

get impatient, roll my dice
double sick is oh so nice

deal me with a blood red heart
sticky hand before I start

hiding from blind-woman's buff
if you peek, you'll find it rough

who stuck a tail on her ass?
don't ask, I think he'll pass

Bob's your uncle, open eyes
dusty bin, a sanitary prize

I get sick of all the clues when
dear Miss Scarlet's bound to lose

as my compere sits here waiting
feel the jackpot hesitating

I could name this song in four
bingo-crawling on the floor

is this my monopoly
of the board-game P.M.T?

Feather-Lite

Rubbery – oh, vile rubber song
Gasping, sucking, not love
The snap of a slippery grip
Some sort of odious glove

I'm dry but wet inside my head
The blood begins to flow
A drum, you bang a chafing beat
You cease? How do I know?

The pack I spy, inside the white
Two left, I cannot hide
It bursts, you laugh, a wicked tap
That drips, perhaps you never tried?

Feminism Under Threat

She, no sister of mine,
with her fussy insistence on a doily for each
and her proud display of china with pink roses.
But please don't call them red, or drop crumbs,
for then she will snarl, this will spoil her day and she
will have to hoover around and under your guilty feet.

She squats, lips tight, ready to strike
at any threat to her carefully constructed nest,
provided for her when once she smiled,
promised warmth and suspenders -
She doesn't obey, but masquerades, passive,
to the outside world...

Inside her territory, she sulks, cries and behold:
another freezer, microwave, or dishwasher.
These hallowed symbols of possession mean
less work, in or out of the feathered enclosure,
but she doesn't understand why I, his daughter,
have been on benefits for some time now...
Yet he cannot, or will not, disentangle himself
from her safe, suffocating web,
long enough to reach out to his family
before her entrance -

Their photographs under lock and key,
she winces if their names pass his lips.
She has managed to make me disregard
my cultivated ideas of female oppression.
This, no man has ever succeeded to do,
as she destroys my precious feminist cloak
with a single, scorching glance.

Indecision

Feast now for my evensong
Pallid maiden for too long

Wait now until my dawn
Playing babies on the lawn

Time waits for no woman
Nature's own fertility van

Child mothers push and smile
As the men hide single file

Cling to foamy, dreamy sponge
All my school-friends take the plunge

Twenty-six and now my eggs
Cluster round between my legs

Nightmares of a swelling life
Tremble as I see the knife

Hold off time for just one hour
While I hide in age-old tower

Rescue me with unsure rope
Give an unborn child some hope

Milk Of Human Kindness

My milk, previously cream, has turned sour
I have no more nutrition for you
Instead of steadfastly feeding, I cover
My breasts, noting they have now turned blue

The cold has frozen all warmth to ice
The milk of human kindness has dried
There's no longer incentive to be nice
My ability to nurture has died

I'm no longer lit by an inner sun
The flames were extinguished by unseen fingers
My soul as inviting as the habit of a nun
You ask if any human feeling lingers

I have eternally watched men kill and maim
Seen humankind torture and torch each other
I am sick; surely you would feel the same
I relinquish my post as the universal mother

Mine's A Microgynon

a dull ache was beating
just as I started eating

a sugar-tasting bitter-sun
the liberal, facile valium

imagination, it's only that
I'm swollen and it's not fat

and where had I chosen
to have my feelings frozen?

headache - just the tension
I was not supposed to mention

day after year, green or blue
swallow and lay back for you

I salivate at a gloomy sight
the enemy crackles, out goes the light

who deceives who? I asked him again
my enlarged breasts took all the strain

my hypocrite hero cultivates still
a traitor's belief in the mystical pill.

My Hot Tip For World Cup '94

Baggio Romeo, Baggio Verona
Merge dreamily in female minds
With cornettos and other favourite things

The Mediterranean sun kisses darkly
On the pitch, on a gondolier
With glittery love-dust

Mothers and Madonnas hold out crucifixes
Buddha and Jesus view them with wry amusement
Both having endowed them with god-like strength

The civil war is forgotten this year
As they battle with Spain and Brazil
Even the referee is on their side

Her mind is on the score-line
Yet also on blue piercing skies and eyes
Penetrating through glad-women's thighs

Venice, Florence and Rome nestle in LA
A pocket of red-bloodied wine
The women of England cast a lazy eye
And cheer

Limbs of Apollo, Zeus and Venus
A sensuous threesome, the Italian trinity
Another Veronian hat-trick.

Mystique

Ah! I blanche and slide away
under one's bustle, so furtive today
no-one explained my female growth
heavens untimely, oh how I loathe
my feelings, my sin I will not show
Eve's rotten maggot, starting to flow
tinkle piano, my feminine charms
drift anaemically in his arms
needing him to avoid my gutter
on with confetti, a nervous flutter
corset I open, festered inside
blood spot horrific for a new bride
damaged, soiled, do send me back
muster his troops, a moral attack
inherent legacy, all is too pale
he made me delicate, he cannot fail.

Supermodel

There is a female, as thin as my windpipe
She's a woman-child, who will never be ripe
Moon-saucer eyes, the depth of a puddle
Vomit-eat-vomit, leaves guts in a muddle

Those silicone mounds may descend to the belly
No matter, as long as they glisten on telly
She, of course, is involved in serious concerns
Spouting world issues, as she twirls and earns

She cannot, must not, gain one inch
Doomed to trip in death-traps that pinch
A slack-jawed actor needs a starring role
So he swathes her stick-arms in a fox-fur stole

He looks convinced, integrity intact
As her collagen lips say, 'I really *can* act'
Mankind worships her, wreathes her in flowers
We shuffle, we bloat, as above us she towers

The Sacrifice

I saw you in a purple swirl
Feminist woman, suffragette girl
Placards and violence you made your life
No longer were you content as a wife

I laughed with derision and turned away
Not knowing that you'd convert me one day
I saw you in pictures and in my dreams
I glimpsed the horse, then heard your screams

Oh, girls of the eighties, independent and free
I died for you, but you refused to see
Sexual harassment, rape and violence
And despite my sacrifice, still suffer in silence

You left me so quietly, no ranting or wailing
But you left me chained to the feminist railing

The Fly, Psychobabble And Nirvana

Despite my horrendous first day at the therapeutic community, due to an unfortunate encounter between my ear canal and a fly, I decided I would give it another go.

So I did. And I soon settled into some kind of routine, which, despite my sack-full of neuroses, I found strangely comforting.

At 10.00am, the group session kicked off. Caroline still did that jiggling and yawning thing, though no-one took any notice. Then she stormed out, muttering under her breath how everyone hated her, it was all a waste of time and what was she doing here.

With that over, silence reigned. Sometimes, I would catch Peter's eye and we would try not to laugh, but quite often one of us, or both of us, would crack. Of course, this irritated some people who were so paranoid they thought we were laughing at them. This could be awkward. The most paranoid person, who two minutes before had seemed quiet and nicely drugged up, would turn into a rottweiler and attack us for our insensitivity to their obvious distress. The invigilator would naturally ask them what they were upset about. By this point, there was about two minutes to go. However, the distressed person would start to pour out their feelings, only to be cruelly cut short by the invigilator's call that time was up.

Some people went straight to the TV, to watch `Kilroy' or something mindless. Caroline would reappear and sit in front of the programme, no longer yawning but still swinging her leg, slightly less frantically.

Others of us, including myself and Peter, would gravitate towards the tiny smoking room. Or smoking cupboard, as it was known. Peter and I would fall about laughing and others would half-heartedly reprimand us. Peter and I would then have a conversation, shutting everyone else out as far as we could. I would tell Peter about my motor neurone disease, or whatever it was I thought I had that day. Peter commiserated and then generally proceeded to tell me about some disastrous night out he'd had with some dodgy sounding bloke, which had invariably ended with him coming home alone wretched, when he would then get even more off his face than he already was. He would then usually offer me some valium, which he had a seemingly endless supply of. It would have been churlish to refuse. Why hadn't we mentioned any of this in the group? Well, there are some things that are private, aren't there?

So that was how the large group continued. Until, that is, the day Suzanne joined us. As we got our first look at her, alarm bells went off. Her face was beetroot-blotchy. Bang on at 10.01 am, Suzanne started to cry, telling us about her dead fiancé. God, of course it was terrible. Awful. We all felt incredibly sorry for her. Yes, we all listened. Intently. For the full hour. To be honest, we were partly relieved that someone other than Caroline had appropriated the silence. Out of respect, even Peter and I avoided even glancing in each other's direction.

However, afterwards in the smoking cupboard (Suzanne didn't smoke) some old-hand suggested that it was looking like the statutory weeper had arrived. What did they mean? I naively asked. They told me that, in this type of set up, there's always someone who cries all the time. I was dubious. We continued to discuss amongst ourselves how likely it was that Suzanne would behave the same way the next day. Some of us, me included, said that as it was her first day, we should give her the benefit of the doubt. Others expressed their opinion that she was 'leopards don't change their spots'. Pessimistic? Realistic? Well, time would tell, wouldn't it? Time always does.

The next morning, our curiosity was so piqued that we all, for once, arrived on time. Suzanne was already in situ, ominously clutching a handful of tissues.

10.01. Suzanne starts weeping copiously. In between sobs, she continued to extol her fiancés virtues. We let her carry on. And on. She's grieving, I thought. Please, let's give her a chance.

10.59. Suzanne is still crying and gulping. The invigilator, looking embarrassed, called time.

Back in the smoking room, the pessimists told us optimists that they had told us so. She was going to be the weeper.

And sob she did. Every day. The whole hour. By Friday, we were all exhausted. So too was Stephen, the invigilator, who, poor bastard, had drawn the short straw and had the unenviable job of being Suzanne's counsellor. He was a decent bloke; funny, perceptive and he looked like one of `The Proclaimers'. But not today, he didn't. He looked deathly white, seemed to have suddenly developed grey hairs and had violet circles under his eyes.

At 9.45am, he suddenly sighed and asked - pretty damn sharply for him - whether Suzanne was remotely interested in anyone else's problems. She momentarily stopped howling, looked around astonished, then asked angrily whether anyone else had experienced such a horrendous time. Many had, or something similar. But no-one spoke. So she hiccupped and went on and on...

Then, there was another new arrival: Tony, who showed no signs of being a leg swinger, or a crier. He didn't speak at group, but then no-one other than Suzanne ever did.

Afterwards, I found Tony in the smoking room. I decided to forego my usual cosy chat with Peter, so that I could welcome Tony to the community. I liked him immediately. He seemed kind, funny and strangely normal. The only thing about him that seemed unusual was his red, cracked hands. Being naturally nosey, I asked him if he had an allergy. I had loads and could happily talk about them for hours. But no. It was the cleaning, he explained. Apparently, he cleaned. All the time. All his benefit money was spent on cleaning materials. Aggy and Kim would have loved him. Getting out of his front door was torture, because all he wanted to do was to be back inside, scouring and scrubbing until his hands bled. I revealed my little quirks and we found a source of comfort in each other's foibles.

A couple of things occurred. Tony went for an HIV test. Myself, Peter and Tony all waited for the results, getting more and more worried as the day dawned for his results. But he came back from the clinic ecstatic, for him. He was negative. We all went out for a drink that evening to celebrate Tony's good news. Little did I know that evening how Tony's result would rebound on my own life.

Tony also had another effect on the group as a whole, which revealed itself just after his test results. It was in group therapy. Suzanne was, as ever, whining on and snivelling. Suddenly, there was a roar of anger from Tony. He told Suzanne that he had felt so angry and disturbed after yesterday's session that he had been up all night, trying to scrape away her negative energy. He ended by yelling that she needed to know how fucking ill she had made him feel. This was a breakthrough. Everyone had been thinking exactly what he had just articulated. The floodgates were open. We were all screaming at her, telling her about the impact she had had on all of us. The adult tiny tears doll just looked bewildered. But she had stopped crying. Just for five minutes. But did she stop crying in the future? Did she fuck. But finally we all felt we had the right to challenge her behaviour. And that was progress.

And what of me whilst this was going on? Was I any better and had the health panics diminished at all? Were there any signs that I would recover?

For a start, I couldn't do that disgusting thing with my nose. I would pick it until I it bled like a pig with its throat cut. Not that I'd ever seen one. It was just one of my anxious compulsions, like checking under my arms for swollen lymph glands. I would bleed so profusely that I decided I needed a blood transfusion. But of course, it was well known that all blood transfusions were still tainted with the HIV virus. Oh yes, they might say that all blood was pure now. But I knew better. It was all a Tory conspiracy to kill us all off to save money on the NHS. So I panicked even more.

The other thing that being at the centre all day meant was that I could no longer live on the doorstep of the casualty department at Guy's hospital. I was a well-known feature there and wouldn't have been surprised if I hadn't become one of the capital's tourist attractions. The staff's reactions to me varied. One Doctor was always kind, telling me gently, time and time again, that no I didn't have ME, MS or any other initials except - he hinted, possibly OCD. Another more vicious Doctor hated my guts, and refused to see me. She also had the gall to send a letter to my GP, informing him I was a neurotic time-waster and asking why he couldn't control my behaviour better. My GP read this out to me in an attempt to make me confront the consequences of my actions. Or some psychobabble crap. I thought it was excessively harsh. Strangely my GP seemed to have some kind of sympathy for this Doctor, though I had no idea why.

So yes, there had been a couple of changes. No nose picking and no more trips to casualty, because I had such a busy life at the centre and had made lots of new friends. But I didn't feel much better.

However, the day of my ward arrived. This will be where the treatment will really start. I would now reap the rewards of attending this place daily. Richard, my Psychiatric nurse, the psychiatrist and the head honcho, Professor Mapp, all came together for a couple of hours to discuss me - the results of which I was to be informed of, after they had decided what the hell they could do with me. They seemed to be taking as long as Guy's hospital's casualty department took to see me. God, how the time was dragging. But maybe that was a good sign?

Finally, I was called in. They were all there. Except it was a different shrink. The previous sadist, John, had finally fucked off, though not before he had made one final push to send me over the edge. As soon as I stepped into the room, I knew I had made another schoolboy error. He asked me how the fly was. I told him I had drowned it in some oil and it was down the sink. He laughed sarcastically and made it clear that I had not seen the fly at all, dead or otherwise and my reaction was psychosomatic. So, was I, in his view, psychotic or not? He answered in the negative, but added that I had a highly vivid imagination. My Mother was always told that in my school reports, so there was nothing new there. Exactly how much taxpayers' money had been wasted training this tosser?

My next move was pointless, but I was feeling crap and thought I had nothing to lose. I offered him a look at my traitorous mole, which had apparently gone black overnight, for his delectation. He asked me how on earth I had managed to see it at all and asked if I was a contortionist. I reluctantly told him about all the mirrors, which made him crease up with laughter for ages. After he had stopped chortling, he asked me how I would feel if the mole was cancerous and the tentacles of the cancer were spreading through my body, devouring all my organs in their wake. I was shaken, but had wised up by this time. I told him I wasn't allowing him to use me to fuel his sick predilections. Then I walked out and for a final shot, I told him I really pitied his next set of patients and that it was a real tragedy, because he may actually have been a caring person at one point. I slammed the door after me for effect. I am sure he was really, really scared by that.

He had been replaced by one of the nicest men I have ever met. You would never know he was a shrink. I never knew his real name, but we all called him Inglebert. I think he was Danish. Danes are brilliant. Did you know they were the only country during World War 2 to save practically all their fellow citizens of Jewish extraction? No other nation achieved half this goal. How fantastic is that? Recently, they have made the best TV thriller ever. 'The Killing'. Now, that is what I call therapy. Sorry - I digress. But watch it, if you get a chance.

I had already visited Inglebert several times. The first day I went in, tentatively clutching my throbbing head. I clearly had a brain tumour at the very least. He informed me that he really shouldn't be fuelling my health panics, but he could tell me that brain tumours hardly ever started with headaches. After that, when I went in with a new panic, even if he had refused me that oh so very temporary relief, I always came out feeling better.

He had even suggested a new medication, as he thought my current anti-depressant rather `over stimulating' for someone with panic attacks and high levels of anxiety. I had tried it, but spent a horrendous night having panic attack after pain attack. I informed him the next morning that I wasn't ever touching that evil concoction again. He observed calmly that some of the panic may have been as a result of my anxiety, but he certainly wasn't going to insist I continue to take it. I actually did try the same medication years later and despite the awful initial side-effects, it eventually worked remarkably well. So Inglebert, if you are reading this, which I seriously doubt, you got it right after all.

Yet another digression. Back to the ward round. Professor Mapp started by saying I had settled in well. He asked if Gary was being supportive at home and I replied that he wasn't and that it was Gary's fault I was in this state anyway. Professor Mapp remarked that I seemed to be harbouring a great deal of resentment. Too fucking right I did. The Professor continued by saying that I needed to work hard at this and at the root cause of all my anxieties with Richard, in an attempt to try to get to the root cause of all my fears and obsessions. But I couldn't function in a therapeutic sense (ah yes, more psychobabble) until my health panics were under control. What was proposed was that I pick a Doctor in whom I trusted (are you kidding?) and make a list over the ensuing two weeks with of all my health concerns noted. I could then go through the list with the Doctor. I would find, Dr Mapp added, that these troublesome thoughts would diminish with time. Everyone in the room nodded sagely. Except me. As the monumental consequences of this pronouncement sank in, I started to shake so violently I nearly fell off my chair. Two weeks. I couldn't hold on for two days. I tried to push for a week. But it was apparently non-negotiable and did I need some water?

I staggered out, bewildered and terrified. Peter asked me how it had gone, but I couldn't speak. He silently shook out a massive handful of valium and went and got me a cup of tea. So that's all they could do for me? I had expected so much more - wanted something miraculous. And this is what I get. Two weeks? Horrific. Jesus, God help me.

Thankfully, there was soon an event that was so profound it was almost enough to take my mind off the two week thing. Though not quite, obviously.

I remember the day he arrived, because it was the day Pip took all her clothes off in the group. She had ripped off her jumper and t-shirt to reveal *surprisingly large breasts. She was dancing sinuously, and laughing, whilst discarding her clothes provocatively. He was the first person to shout for someone to bloody well cover her up. The (male) invigilator finally awoke from his stupor and managed to tear his eyes off Pip in order to shield her quite remarkably firm boobs from our fascinated gaze.*

After group, I intended to congratulate him on his presence of mind. But he was sitting in the corner of the smoking room that was my place. Peter gave me a worried look. He knew I was in a shit mood because of the mouth cancer (which was definitely no ordinary ulcer). I strode purposefully over and started to tell him to fuck off out of it. But he had his walkman on. How bloody rude. As I sat down opposite him, waiting for him to unplug himself, I casually studied him. Black, nice looking, He was wearing a striped t-shirt and black jeans, together with some pretty decent biker boots. But obviously a complete wanker. I betted myself he was listening to some R & B shite. Or rap. It didn't occur to me then that these were racist preconceptions.

He finally tore himself away from whatever the hell he was listening to and rudely asked me what I wanted. I was a bit perturbed. How was it that I was suddenly a source of annoyance to him? I congratulated him on his actions in the group. He just shrugged. I was about to walk away, when something made me ask him what he was listening to. He told me it was Nirvana. I tried to stay cool, but with minimal success. I loved Nirvana, but didn't know anyone else that gave a shit when Kurt Cobain shot his brains out. Gary thought Kurt was a selfish cunt and so was anyone who committed suicide. There's empathy for you, I had replied after this sweeping denouncement.

I asked this rather interesting man which album he preferred. 'In utero.' It would be, wouldn't it? Out of the corner of my eye, I could see Peter imperceptibly shaking his head. I just ignored him. When did I ever do what anyone told me? Besides, this was all, well, intriguing. So what was his favourite track, I asked, dreading the reply. But wanting it too.

`Frances Farmer Takes Her Revenge on Seattle'.

The meaning of those lyrics, that describe the real story of a Hollywood actress who was locked up in an insane asylum for being too politically outspoken, was not lost on either of us. Kurt used to sing it onstage dressed in a straightjacket. Which was, as I explained to this strange boy, why it was also my favourite.

We smiled at each other. Ours was the smile of complicity. His was the smile of a devil. So, this was where the real psychosis was. And I needed more….

The Ruby Desire I Keep For You

A Valentine From Berlin

What a funny valentine,
hiding my hide behind
a bush, my anti-greying
and your continued greying -
Perhaps our combined planet is too old.
It used to be Eden green and our coiled
guts, our intestines, were as one.
I have a gripe, I think our colons interact.
But do you feel my clenching?

I hear codeine is good to stop
this vengeful yearning for a
subliminal solution for ills.
There's pills, but nothing bitten yet.
(How German, how Nazi - they are now us,
as we were then - but better.)
Berlin - we'll sort it out in
Berlin - leave your jackboots at home.
Berlin - don't fixate - it's Tolstoyan times.

We'll goosestep in spirit,
waving the flag of white Prussian peace.
Stay in the Fritskratzenburg Inn.
Are we to stay alienated on our own map?
You are a tall wall to climb, but you
were my flagship. Where are the
pre-war boundaries? Is there a wire where
I end? Is my head your territory?
Tanks, wanks, whatever - it's boys stuff.
Or so I am told.

Pity that I threw my red feminist rag
to those bull-dykes long ago.
This is no democratic Duma.
How has our Soviet turned autocratic?

Ra-Ra Rasputin Rap,
spattered in a rat-red trap.
Tsarist shrink to a Cherie-like sap,
healed a haemophiliac.
God the Devil wouldn't die.

Anyway, depleted child cells
still spilled. Maroon mapping
of the end of the old world.

All that thinning, watery blood,
leached from Europe's imperialism.
The victorious overthrow of corruption.
Poverty sucked at the world of the pearl-dripping,
toe-tipping Romanovs. When they were slaughtered,
they threw starved earth into
their bunker - but some were still alive.

Them, their siblings - squealing, spitting soil, singing
to their unknown Christian children. Hatred, hierarchy; yes -
But their pitiful prayers still echo.
Where was the holy trinity then?
The Death Hymn. Her as Mary, God as Man,
as Jesus, as Jehovah, Mohammed, Buddha.
Was it always sliced up with songs of slavery?
Is a testament truth? Is history, is our story,
ever black, white, sepia?

We've marched with Marx through Moscow,
paraded our politics in Paris.
No more war, peace, more bread, dignity,
equality, fraternity.....
(We were always out of step - you outpace me.
When I fall into my own rhythm, you yank my chain.
I have no liberty.)

Let's forget. I am Trotsky.
I feel so obliterated. Blackout.
Let me jostle like a young blood
into your barricaded brain.
I am so sick of this gender war.

Where shall we meet when
the Earth turns electric?
Are we still in love? We were always so eclectic.
We used to be able to take any song,
any poem and book and agree.

We should use this as a peace proposal, at least.

My siren screams out.
We must get our belongings packed.
We are only allowed the basics, I believe,
but let's try to smuggle some
champagne to our bunker.
Leave behind your tear-blitzed manifesto.
It was always too sulphuric.

But perhaps we should
grab our snaps from Egypt.
Me posing at the pyramids, symbols of
yet another kind of oppression.
I am half smiling, half scared, oblivious to the middle East's own
Berlin wall. The Egyptians would soon throw off the
shackles of this - their own Apartheid.

Evolutions, revolutions, resolutions.
We whirl, nauseous, round this
germ-warfare groove.
A cyclical path without glory.
You have a chance to grab me before I
get lost amongst the ants, scattering
as the anthrax finally descends.

Oh - let's make our peace,
before the world sinks, scarred, like
a shriven, bloodless heart.

Alien

You recline and lazily close your eyes.
I watch your eyelashes descend
and wonder what planet you are on,
or what you took last night to
make you drift so dreamily...

You have walked straight out of
one of your sci-fi movies that I,
as you know, find tedious, into
my bookish, feminist mind.
I don't know what you are doing,

inhabiting this strange environment.
I want to beam you up somewhere,
see you dissolve in rays of moonshine;
but I know, if you are abducted,
it will not be by me.

Another Day

Sheaves of dark, subtle as your kiss
Interweave between sudden bliss

Morning brings warmth and hidden tears
Can your mouth obliterate my fears?

I walk out the door, from hazel to brown
Submerged in confusion, I start to drown

When your voice fades, I begin to cry
And he looks at me and wonders why -

Soiled love brings pity and so I stay
As we cling together for another day...

Colours

Black, cancerous creep;
you said that I was racist.
You boxed bright, shiny,
your face oily with resentment.
Your breath greased
my slippery conscience.
Your pores oozed empathy
onto my grunge-loosened loins

I saw only that your demerara skin
matched the brown of your eyes.
I overlooked that they
zig-zagged a red-currant hell.
Personality? I glanced green-like
and ignored the word disorder.

You know the gypsy
you said you saw?
She saw you, all right,
glistening in your own
gold-sovereign grime.
Did she know already how
your cigarette burns bubbled
bodily fluids onto my future?

Your self-lacerations were
mauve malignancies, bunched
together in my head –
as contagious as syphilis.
When you quartered me, you
seemed to cauterise temporarily.

Then, suicide sirens sang
blue in my veins,
reverberating past white
offenders, beds – You
chalked up grey victories when
they fed you intravenously –
You dribbled out your
charcoal childhood just for me.

My pink-cream hands
shook with culpability

I sluiced your sludge-liver
with concern – sliced it
full of juice and vitamins,
prayed it would hold, collapse.
My faith teetered between
life and dark,
until dying twice became
as commonplace as
a Flanders graveyard.

Funny how your tragedy
eventually made me smile.
Strange how my
pity paled pastel.
Honestly, I sponged you
over and out.
You grew insignificant –
until your tears finally
had no colour.

Dave

You and I, ripped apart,
blood washing away love,
sin rinsing me clean,
but leaving you with scar tissue,
easily healed by your scorn.

The needle-strewn past
erased our days of calm.
Drop upon drop of citric
acid could never be tender,
as my stomach churned
and my senses dimmed...

and didn't we both forget
to throw away the syringe?

Dead But Not Forgotten

I was unaware, at the time,
that we both existed
in our own tortuous bubbles.
We laughed, loved and lied for a while,
clinging to each other with razor claws.
When you escaped, you got torn to shreds.
I melted into a puddle of self-pity and anger.
I can't forget you hated me when you died.
It distresses me we couldn't make amends.
Wherever you are, I will find you.
Sometimes, I feel compelled to join you.
We can both float on our own tortuous clouds,
loving, laughing and lying.

Dreaming

Wilfred Owen still makes me cry
The smell of the sea evokes a sigh

Dreams of white windmills slowly spin round
And there's something I'd lost, but suddenly found

The take-off prior to puffball clouds
Stillness and peace, after the crowds

The things that I think are mine to do
And the ruby desire I keep for you

The pillow was wet from a lost nightmare
But now I can dream, when I know you are there

Gone In A Heartbeat

(for Mark)

You never said sorry
for the German girl
with the plum-coloured hair.
She was up and down you
like quicksilver.

What an accomplished
contortionist - you bent over
backwards for her,
like you once did for me.

It was as though I had never
felt your quick heart hard
in my ears, beating for me alone,
but too rapidly for your own good.

Everywhere, anywhere, I saw you -
I clutched at your coat. You thought
there was no end
to my self-abasement.

Until, finally, I lay listening to a
different heartbeat. I think you knew.

The final glance I gave you
was one of indifference.
I dismissed you with a twitch
of the hips you once worshipped.

How was I to know the
clanking cauldron of my jealousy
had continued to warm your blood?

I still try to imagine your last night,
swallowing assorted pills with
your characteristic recklessness -
not caring what the
outcome would be.

You and I - together, apart.
No heartbeat has ever thrummed
under my skin like yours.

Green

Fair, cantankerous, luminous youth
It nearly took mine to discover your truth

A white sculptured face, impression of sallow
Eyes glazy pools, were you really so shallow?

Often I gave you a cloying incense
Spitting a cough, you burned too intense

Bottle green cherubim, not meant to be
I waved at the door, you never did see

Leafy life tender, bright burning sky
We lay on the grass and said, *what if I die?*

Pills, scattered teabags, they made us too old
I looked in your window, they said you were sold

The clash they crashed, we're strangers now
I painted my clown's face and gave you a bow

Finality shifted to your satellite head
Why do I shriek when they say punk is dead?

You wasted and throttled me, so I could live
Forever too young, I have no wreath to give

Monsoon

You are my perpetual dark cloud.
I know you have no silver lining.
Your stormy head makes mine whirl.
A hurricane is tossing us around.
Your lightning crackles across the room,
igniting my senses. Sparks flash from
my eyes into and through your body.
The weather seems to be so changeable,
but today I am drenched in the
warm, clammy outpouring of your monsoon -
This sensual soaking is something I want
to embrace, but dare not -
Could it be I am finally turning my back
on Summer's wonderland?

My Poems

I have been cramping with the birth struggle.
Now I have new infants, squalling and
sour, they all have the same volcanic whine.
I tend them anyway, hush them as they
screech. You look at them, dismally, drearily.
You are proud but sad, conceived as they were
through a surgical gown-gloom.

I wish there was one more inside me, to pull
from the pink, bright me of hearts and harvests.
It would be perfect and smiling, a replica of
you and me, when I am sunset-sheen.

I could hand it to you and
it would say everything golden
that I have left unsaid and unborn.
You could swaddle the best of me.
My hair tied up to show the nape of
my neck, which you love to kiss, when it doesn't
smell of smoke. The laugh you love to see, but too often do not.
The arch of my shoulders when they are not knotted with anxiety.
My most tender caress of you. I want to translate these thoughts
and deliver them, without even the need for gas and air,
through me, to you.
For you.

Night Dragons

Tonight,
she sees her hand looped,
suspended, touching her head.
Her cardboard cut-out rises up,
looks unconcerned from the ceiling,
drifts back with unease to her body.
This body imagines a drawing,
coloured blue where her ice lies,
or red where patches are burning -
she saw it in a yellowing magazine...

Now, for one crystal spot of time,
she feels like Christopher Robin,
dreams of fighting dragons
and feels so
very sleepy...
but slays too soon - and it's he
that is Christopher and she is
the dragon that she fights,
so she creeps on down the bed,
collects scars where kisses fade,
loving and wrestling, sleepless again,
until tonight.

Red

You and I,
my split ends twirling
around your finger -
I singed them only yesterday,
now you got burned too.

After my fourth glass of wine,
I got to like you when you talked,
as your eyes misted with emotion.
You told me that you never cried,
but I saw you and made it happen.

I think, what you'll do now,
is go into a bar, then another -
the one where you saw me -
and you'll pace around, with flowers
for a blonde, then offer them to someone else.

But try to avoid the flame next time,
because I'm coppery and dangerous
and will not say go,
as I'm stuck on red -
for the moment.

Resurrection

You thought you had destroyed me -
didn't you?
But my grave is as shallow as
you once were.

So I will rise,
my hair aflame with
glow-worms of revenge.

Obscenities shooting from
my dead-chalky lips,
covering you with ash.

My bile flying,
burning your uppity tongue.

One glare from this vitriolic vixen
will flash Zyclon-B into
those metallic-blue eyes,
leaving hollow black.

Blinded. But you won't forget
the sight of me,
this time around.

Your gravest error was
to categorise me as
sub-human.

How long my nails have grown
in this blood-moistened earth.

They are talons to tear you
and your fucking swastika
into curdled critters,
fit only for the ravens.

No grieving widow.
No keening or wailing.
My spittle will sear you to hell.
Straight to hell, boy.

My will
be done.

Sunday

Sunday afternoon, the world has closed down
I am swathed in grease, in his dressing gown

He plays games in a park - so carefree
I bloat, I vomit and hate this side of me

There is nowhere accessible on earth right now
But I ring, you answer - and it's right somehow

Everywhere is shut, but you answer my call
And somewhere is open, after all.

The Return

Watching a mauve dusk dry your hair
Sensing its curl looping your neck
Feeling your voice through a yellowing heat
Looking as your body negotiates the world

The lie of your linen shirt on your shoulders
A few straying chest hairs scrambling upwards
Your shoes still turn inwards, sharing old secrets
Those soulful fingers can soothe like strong cats

A metallic mask is shed, like skin
You have returned to my senses, complete

Twelve Years

Fluffy dream-clouds that July,
being blown in by billow-breeze.
It lazily stroked our pillowed, welded heads,
your striped towel hanging -
a sign for me that some things may,
or may not, be eternal.

Then, adrift on love's isolated island,
we climbed in through a window open wide,
wild laughing and stumbling and
clothes tumbling; I recall you had left
your birthday cake in a bar, in which we
had drunk endless strawberry rum kisses
and each other's velvet ears
on crimson-cushioned sofas...

We lived in Victoria-land for days, weeks -
too wrapped up to change the record,
too submerged in passion's sweet lava,
paying homage to each other's eyes -
and all the while, I would ask,
can this last?

Only yesterday, I discovered
that Summer is only ever
two heartbeats away.

My Days With An Opium-Eater

I thought I was safe in our serene sunflower summers, but you soon found stronger seasons could replace me. Yes, you still cared - through an ochre-opium haze, which seemed to expunge demons I never knew existed. Your caressed me with your eyes shuttered and opened mine.

I had read Burroughs, De Quincy; knew all the words to all the thrillingly hip and decadent songs of the Velvet Underground. Scrutinising Edie Sedgwick's factory life, way before Sienna Miller. Hearing your friends talking in low, slow voices. So I knew. I tried flushing you out. Throwing the stuff out to sea. Pleading with you.

All for nothingness, rinsed out by your blood. It left us with such scar tissue, purple ropes of it that we could not untangle. Your needle strewn daze. Drop upon drop of citric acid. Burning our sunflower past in a heated spoon. Acrid can never be tender. My stomach churned as my senses dimmed. I realised I could not be a moth to your flame.

Breaking through trashing waves of brown-gold fluid, I found me again. Then there was him: I looked into his clear, hazel eyes, flecked with a beauty I hadn't recognised before. My brick-dust heart melted, molten. Then your quick sand smile faded. The docile, never - asking questions - me, threatened to desert our garden.

By now, thorns and nettles had made it impenetrable. You had been too obsessed by poppy seeds to prune and reap. You pretended to come clean. Said you would reform. Those same old promises. Guilty for leaving you - I tried a final shot of your future in your arm. Lifeless. You had become a desert with no oasis in sight. Not in my lifetime. Only caramel - camel tracks there. No healing fluids.

You had grown too sulphuric in your quagmire, too swampy to infiltrate. My soil is now fecund spring with daffodils and his sweet herb garden. But sometimes, I still wonder why you didn't throw away your syringe.

The Yellow World Of Smoke And Curious Faces

A Chemical Reaction

The chemicals emanating from my brain
are not the same as yours, oh no.
Mine, of course, cancerous-like,
reaching parts of my body
I was unsure existed.

Tomorrow, I may be paralysed,
unable to flicker even one eyelid.
Yesterday, my heart stopped beating
long enough for me to hope
I had finally died and was in purgatory,
rather than this current hell.

Your eyes correctly assimilate the sun;
I can see it in your smile.
My vision is full of thunder.
I have an inbuilt sunshine filter.

When lightning strikes, it will jolt
me from sadness into despair.
My misery apparatus is at full throttle;
your hormones keep you in contentment.
Imagine my envy.

As Usual

Unbelievably, I find myself enduring the unendurable.
I cannot comprehend how one eye blinks and waters,
or how one leg eases in front of the other,
slowly but surely.
I am astonished as my bladder empties itself
in the appropriate place
and gawp in amazement when I find myself on
the right train.
If I answer the phone in a tone that can be
described as sane,
then it becomes an object of incredulity
and I grip it like some holy icon, pray to it,
wipe my lipstick from the mouthpiece...
It's true, I can work the photocopier and it hums
as though the humming in my head were normal.
Everything works just as usual -
the only abnormality is me, wondering
how?

At The Ear Nose And Throat Hospital

I was in the darkened booth, grey pavlovian rat.
I pressed the required button, ear mufflers inverting
my fear. Then spin-screech chair rocks. This astronaut
contraption flying me to planets petrified.

Red light winks, surely my eye blinks, as I try to count
backwards, breathing black oxygen intermittently.
The old woman knitting by the machine initially lulled me,
but her pace and her blood has quickened.

I forget where I am, though I know it is some
mad-mice mausoleum.

It's over, the technician said. I'm finished.

I gagged.

Branwell Clinic

I entered the yellow world
of smoke and curious faces,
clutching my poetry
and vitamin pills, shortly to be confiscated.
(We don't encourage pill-popping of any kind here.)

I kept the poetry, but the words scrambled,
so instead I played dominoes
with sweet-faced Patrick, who may have been 55 or 75.
He had dried out more times than a shoreline in Summer;
his shakes tumbled the dominoes, but still he beat me.

Jason looked as though he belonged to far-off lands –
not Deptford - his emaciated features contorted, as he
sweated through a new drug designed to ease withdrawals,
which was working about as well as Neil's legs -
strong as wood, they splintered under a seizure,
whilst Paul, the ferocious right-wing skinhead,
cradled Neil's head in his lap like a baby
and watched over me, my glowering guardian angel.

We had a barbeque in sub-zero weather
and ran like dizzy deer, kicking a football in the snow,
regaling each other with tales of drug-induced catastrophes,
weak with tears of laughter and guilt...
Who will make it through this scheme of shivery sickness?
we asked each other incessantly

You will - you too, I insisted.

But I was wrong, as the old-hands had predicted.
Not him, not her, despite their protestations
and endurance of pain so severe, they hugged themselves
like their own mothers - continuing to whirl around
the turnstiles of euphoria and desperation.

Me? I left with new poems -
and a new addiction.

Cream Teas And Wasps

I stumbled across myself this July,
glimpsing my hips and an angular smile.
My skin has the pink sheen of cream teas,
but the wasp withholds its sting.

Though my breasts swoop in the heat,
they can swing.

And I buy strings of beads from a red vale of vases.
Sky drifts the fever of pollen, which scatters
and my eyes spangle green palettes of seas.
My freckles look spacey under soda-stream moonlight,
whilst dust races through me in stripes.
The past staggers, a weak buckled colt,
into fuzz tinted grim grimy albums.

This, the minute I stop hedging bets:
today, I discovered my own Indian Summer.

Dear Doctor

I know why it is you cannot meet my eyes
but with a clear conscience you can patronise

Your bedside manner is worse than Crippen's
I am a woman, not something you slip in

You hide behind your prescription pad
and write in my notes, 'this woman is mad'

Your reluctance to give me an explanation
only increases my desperation

It seems we are locked in a silent feud
but you always win, leaving me subdued

Why is it I'm ravaged with shame
because you have letters after your name?

In case you've forgotten, so have I
so just to spite you, I think I will die

A funeral parlour is a happier place
than your waiting room, where I hide my face

You insensitive man - my own Boris Karloff
I am so stricken - I'd like you struck off

Elixir

I spy the bottle on the wall,
best panacea of them all.
Despite her concern,
I will make my heart burn.
There are no lights on in this town,
as glasses of nothing slip down.
But there's a brightness over there:
the off-licence's heady glare.
It doesn't matter how I pay,
that worry is for another day.

Falling Asleep

As my eyes close, purple forces one slightly open.
Eyes clamped again - eyelids stop pulsing,
as warmth steals through my body -
I claw at the dozy, fractured images that,
in the daytime, signal madness -
now symbols of restoration.
A snatch of lace,
the cracked back of a long-dead crab,
the sinister criss-cross of some twigs,
may descend to an infernal hallucination;
or a face, comfortable with life, can zig-zag
me into hazy rejuvenation -
If I seize good images, they ricochet me
into other peaceful flickerings...
the fuzz of green velvet,
a maroon dog-eared bible,
the sheen of fruit I was unaware existed...
but the terror of non-existence snaps me awake
and the hope of a parallel life,
an escape into better times,
disappears.

Hunted

A viral particle sails through murky air.
It weaves through polluted smog,
hovers above numerous others,
prevaricates, tries to make a decision;
but a whisper from the God of ills
gives it impetus.
It spies me, stumbling from counselling session
to support groups, to the video shop;
senses my vulnerability,
knows my head is crazed with fear,
feels my dread that it may hunt me down.
It circles, swoops vulture-like
into my nostrils; my mouth is gaping.
The bug finds the perfect target,
it has succeeded in its mission -
because tomorrow, I will be sick,
so very sick.

Infectious

You think it is contagious, don't you?
That is why you won't catch my dull eye,
for fear a spark of despondency will set light
to your carefully-combed hair.
If you touch my face, the dread may spread
from my drawn expression to your smug one.

The shabby bleakness of my clothes could,
God forbid, create wrinkles in your smooth attire.
It is possible the persistent quiver in my limbs
affects your posture, giving your stance a slight stoop.

Do you honestly think I need putting into isolation,
when I have accomplished that for myself?

Less Than Nothing

Finest red silk, coarsened black sack
Was the same texture to me

Curled pink smoked-salmon, gritty black blood
Tasted the same to me

The finest-told joke, grim racist gags
Had no effect on me

A sensuous caress, a slash with a knife
Both were painful to me

Earl grey tea, rancid red wine
The same tannin taste to me

Face painted bright, my flat yellow skull
Gave the same reflection of me

Sebastian Faulkes, bland Enid Blyton
Gave the same meaning to me

Little white lies, mouldering untruths
The same old words to me

Serene cypress scent, cloying cologne
Both vile vapours to me

My mother's arms, the poke of a crone
Meant all the same to me

Melody of strings, rubber band pings
The same sharp shock to me

Cool crunchy snow, soot-streaked slime
Felt the same underfoot to me

Skippy salt sea, petroleum puddles
Both watery graves to me

Exuberant existence, dun-coloured death
The same pit, the same tomb
For me.

Self-Analysis

For a while now,
I have been syringing my ears,
examining the contents for
evidence that the wax is me,
mixing it with wine and
sipping amber -
is it brain fluid?

As the new century
crawls, speeds up,
I am scrutinising my sigmoid,
slothful in what it reveals.
I have a CT scan stare,
my analytic apple-eye
stewing in
pancreatic poison.

This quivering, radioactive mole
will not slice open,
rotten with revelations.
Is there anything unlearned
inside my slug-slippery liver,
except the same old pills?
It won't spill and blab,
won't sell secrets to its
tabloid-minded proprietor.

I try to dissect all my organs,
raw juicy gobbets
of insight,
spreading them with
jam-blood on crackers.
I vainly gorge myself,
again and again.

But this incessant introspection,
this eternal sluicing,
the constant consumption
of my navel,
has made me nauseous.

Today, the scalpels sit,
lonely and theatrical,
where they belong:
outside of me -
Life is external.
I walk warm into
the buttercup sun.

September In Norfolk

This room I sit in
should feel peaceful,
the cosy nick-knacks
should calm me -
as I'm nestled here,
cushioned by a house
that has witnessed
no terror, no fear...

I watch the pear-tree lazily
slough its ripe fruit,
detached, lulling me into its boughs
of dreamy greens -
but still, I cannot be
cosseted -
having no layers to shield me -
born raw, without protection,
cruelties still rip through me,
darts of horror still penetrate.

I crack open often,
my insides quivering, pinkly,
for all to witness...
should they dare to look.

Sick Room

He glimpsed her eyes of orange darts
sensed her chalky sick
shut her in with molten dreams
a losing battle, click

Splutter drunk on whitened rooms
a pallid phlegm she'd wheeze
his sob flew in from crying clouds
upon a starch-like breeze

Departure left a lurching drum
ears just missed a beat
thoughts to follow bobbing thread
snapping in the heat

Jigsaw pieces, jagged minds
hers was breaking loose
hot red tongue was burning out
flapping with misuse

Gliding nurse of saddened sheen
let torpid time go, tick
someone soft, but never him
as she was reeling sick

He caught her scent from crumpled sheets
creased, but neatly tossed
she drifted as his sadness clawed
at beauty too soon lost.

The Good Lobe

This lobe, the one on
the extreme left,
is sealed until 2050,
not to be opened
until I have no use for it.

Occasionally, leakage spurts
through the devil's own casing,
oozing hopefully;
grey sludge is good.

The slush of rationality,
the slime of a sap-happy
snail, who trails tirelessly,
trying to spurge a little of
the noble lobe,
the non-schizoid segment
of my head

Throughout,
but over and around it,
the wrapping holds firm.
It is not to be liberated
until consciousness departs.

Wild Woman Of Wonga

This wild Woman of Wonga,
sorceress of dark ages,
witch with a thousand nipples,
vengeful goddess of mythology -
this bitch stalks, arms flailing,
vicious vixen of a scarecrow.
I have repeatedly burnt her.

She is no brave Joan of Arc -
instead she mixes her potions of illogical terrors,
knowing an antidote cannot be found in the woods.
Her banishment is impossible,
as she is slippery in hiding.

Her appearance often takes me unawares -
her face, my face:
she is the me in disguise.

The Day I Dared To Wear Lipstick.

I shifted uncomfortably in my seat. It was about to start. The moment I had been dreading, ever since I received the give-away brown-buff envelope.

"So, you are here," (at which point the man in front of me produced my form as though it were somehow incriminating) "because you say you are depressed. Is this correct?"

I looked up, studying his youngish-old face, his ice-shard, flitting blue eyes, his weak chin, his fluorescent green tie and then around me at what seemed to be some kind of court-room. I was still dazzled by his tie and wondering if my medication was a bit too strong. But clearly not strong enough as, at the sound of his voice, harsh and cold, I started to visibly tremble. Surely he will see I'm an anxiety-ridden wreck.

"Yes, that's absolutely correct, I do," I replied tremulously, though still trying not to sound as though I had lost my wits completely.

This caused him some consternation. "What, you claim to still be depressed, is that right?"

I nodded, or rather wobbled my head somehow, less sure of my ground.

"You have to actually speak, so we have it on record. I repeat, do you still claim to be depressed?"

"Um, yes I do – um, think I am" I replied.

"Well if I am correct and I believe I am, depressed women do not wear lipstick." He nodded, looking delighted at himself. He was really getting into his stride now. "Lipstick, you see," he emphasised happily.

I wondered idly what his rule was if a man wore lipstick. I attempted an answer.

"Well, um, I thought I should make some sort of effort to be..."

"Precisely my point," he interjected, very sharply. God, he was loving this. He should have been born in Germany in the 1930's. The SS would have snapped him up before you could say 'Heil Hitler'.

"If you were actually depressed, you would not have wanted to look nice. Depressed people don't, you see," he explained patronisingly.

The accused, lipsticked mouth fell open, but remained silent, as I tried to think what psychiatric textbook he had somehow misread whilst eating his scrambled eggs this morning. No, he couldn't have even done that.

I was terrified and confused. What would the well me, the unbroken me, have said to this smug, supercilious git to seal his mouth shut for eternity up? To stop him from being let loose onto society? Did he actually remember the words of the hippocratic oath? Did his wife buy that tie? Thoughts careered around my head like a beach-ball in a hurricane.

Then, the old problem reared its head. I am going to.... Oh no, please God, not THAT. It would be too humiliating. I clenched my knees together firmly and tried to deep breathe like my therapist had taught me.

He spoke again, even more sharply. My bladder pulsed alarmingly.

"And what is this you have given me? Let me have a look. So, you are attending a 'therapeutic community.' What on earth is that when it is at home?"

"Um, well, it's a lot of therapy and then you get one-to-one counselling with your…"

"Yes, yes. I don't need to hear the minute to minute details of your day. Why do you have to attend every day? Surely part-time would be sufficient and then you could fit in a job, which would probably be better for you than all the therapy in the world." He preened, stroking his already inflated ego and smiling like a shark. Well, more sneering actually. If sharks sneer.

The feeling of being in front of a firing squad intensified. Can't someone just shoot me, or at least blindfold me?

"And what is this? Yet another letter, I suppose? Oh, it's from a psychiatrist. Let's see what he has to say."

"It's a her," I said, weakly, Perhaps resignation was beginning to set in. I knew what that letter contained, because Dr Schuster had read it out to me, asking me if it would do the trick. At the time, I thought it sounded pretty neat.

"Hypochondrial delusions? Well, well. What will they think of next?"

Sycophantic moans sounded around the ever-shrinking room. I am in some kind of Kafkaesque nightmare and I will wake up soon, I thought. No such luck. He had his audience in the palm of his slimy hand.

"Please explain what this is supposed to mean."

"Well I get these um ideas that I um I have something really seriously wrong with me. Physically, I mean"

"But that's plainly ridiculous. You clearly must know you haven't, otherwise you wouldn't be able to walk here. I have never heard so much nonsense. Psychiatrists. They all need therapy, if you ask me."

Louder laughing. At least, it sounded louder. Yep, the bastard was really on a roll now. There was more to come.

"Do you know you are not seriously ill?"

"On one level I do, but…." Wrong.

"Well, there you are then. I believe you are definitely not depressed and certainly not delusional. You will get my decision by post. Goodbye."

And it was over.

Outside, I lit a cigarette with trembling fingers, knowing it wouldn't help the rampaging lung cancer I was convinced I had (despite an X-ray which my long suffering GP assured me was clear). I looked at the lipstick stained butt and crushed it as though it were that monstrous official's face.

I swiped the lipstick off angrily, surprised to find my face wet. Well, next time I know I won't wear any lipstick. Or next time, I will wear black lipstick. No, there will be no next time. Never again.

I shuffled home like an old beggar, licking wounds that were destined never to heal.

This Is My Posthumous Prose

All The Dead Girls

Did any of us have a sense of foreboding
when we first glimpsed the
imposing Victorian mansion that
was to be our home? Our tomb?

Up some winding stairs, I was
shown a sepia photograph of a
misty-eyed girl wearing a straw boater
and a blouse tucked neatly into
a long skirt. No suffragette she.

`That's Emily - she died ages ago.'
`What happened?'
`Oh, she drowned in the lake.
There's supposed to be a whirlpool
that sucks you in. Which is why it's
strictly out of bounds.'

The next time a girl disappeared,
I knew her. Andrea; glamorous, wild
Andrea. The girl that had hung
a tampax around my teddy's neck.

A ritual lynching for the new girl.
I withheld my homesick tears until
the lights were out and the giggling
had quietened. I had passed Andrea's test.

On my second night, she mysteriously
led me to the dormitory window and - pointing
to the illuminated town - she looked at me,
her face alight with teenage dreams.
`That's where life is, kid. That's where
it's happening. All of it. Everything.'

But Andrea was suddenly not there.
She was spoken about in snatched whispers.
Mentioning her was forbidden.
She had done something unspeakable.
She had died because of it.

And one day, one night, it was my turn.
I was clutching at Andrea's shadow
and had followed the lights.
I had fallen in love with a Scottish lad
from a council estate.

I was locked in the sick bay
because I was so contaminated.
My father arrived, grey
and grim and hurried me out.
I wondered if I should have a blanket
over my head. Or wear a shroud.

Emily, Andrea and I had all died
from our yearnings
and of course, my death
would not be
the last.

Blasphemy

I can no longer avert my eyes from the horrors.
Every agony, every spasm of terror felt
by the incarcerated, the doomed and dying
courses through me, cramping my every movement.

I want to fling myself down and warm the homeless,
burn in the flames with the witches,
breathe the killing air of the gas chambers,
go over the top in the war to end all wars.

It must be possible to step back in time,
erase the fear, stop the world from rotating,
give me the power to stop old people losing their minds,
reverse the dying of small babies who never lived.

Yes, my own pain gives me the right.
Besides, God abandoned his post a long time ago

Dark Ages

The girl and I were profusely sorry
for bumping into each other at the corner.
In case of any misunderstanding,
we both repeated it, emphatically.
She may have been apologetic for being black;
did I feel the guilt of the white oppressor?
Yet, probably neither of us should feel ashamed,
as we've done nothing heinous that we know of,
even though I tick the back of my prescriptions
and perhaps should not.
I am regretful towards my counsellor
for the struggles within my soul.
He is sorry he cannot empathise more.
In these dark ages, we, the forgotten, the blameless,
bow our heads in self-condemnation
and those that should be fuelled with self-loathing
refuse to lighten our burdens
and will never be truly penitent,
or apologise.

Easing Of The Soul

We Protestants have a constant battle of spirit,
as the Catholics protest that they amass guilt.
Despite a burning burden, they are still absolved,
cushioned in the sonorous, sorrowful confessional.

I could embrace the rosary baubles,
glittering goblets and cool absolving crucifixes.
I would worship Mother Mary, Madonna,
inseparable from the inscrutable Mona Lisa.

But instead of Hail Marys, when I have sinned,
I say two Bloodys, three Fucks and a Shit,
as my self-abnegation finds no outlet.
Father, I have committed murder upon my heart.

He is partly oblivious of his crime, Father,
though his twelfth rape sometimes disturbs his sleep.
So the priest offers dreams that soothe him - like cassocks -
providing he practices a few moments of penitence.

But study us, the pathetic Presbyterians,
doomed to wander through streams of self-mutilation,
incarcerated in our tomb-like rectitude,
as they, the holy, gilt-edged ones,
are wrapped in a tomb-like forgiveness.

I can only confess to my diary,
or ask my mother for absolution.
Although she lacks a smug-like serenity,
this must suffice for now.

Knitting Unravelling

(with thanks to Virginia)

You shut clam tight, clamp
your purse mouth, then cycle to
gash gushing fear, alarm.
Oh, God – quick, brakes on.
You're skidding, no hitches, glitches.
Stitch up again with nylon.

Are you flesh? Do I make you crawl?
Do your dreams ever show
the other side? My side and
the inevitable bruised mornings?
If you watch your watch, is it minutes
or days and do you always
slash yellow sun as garters?
Pull up, pull together.
Zip up, brace yourself.
Clench tight now. Button up.

Let no wine whine from your
corked bottle of... what?

Who knows what's there?
Soured, suppurated,
vinegar cider cesspool.
A jacuzzi, you swirl and sizzle,
boiling, bitter. Don't butter yourself.
Overdo yourself, I dare you.

Grill yourself, fry your uppity tongue.
To be rare, to be stripped raw.

Reach yourself. Hold your encased head.
Open that can of...
spaghetti hoops. The children love them,
the little sweets; you should love them
with everything you have.
But you don't rip it open for them.

Where's your pulse, where's your throb
of life? Under armour, sewn into
corseted greying, dead? Your head, heart,
missing, or buried as deep as a grave?
Maybe a tin opener – or a drill.

But maybe you are
already lobotomised through
the self skull turning vice.
You are in a strait-jacket
of your own making.
No dear, it's not me that's mad
(except at 3 in the morning
during the Godless hours: stroke, strike at 5).

Hum all you like,
the tuneless are lunatics.
Knit as chattering inane
as you like,
but you are coming undone.

One-Armed Combat

I heard the sound of one hand clapping
The other arm shot in some war
I saw the eyes of reason snapping
Age-old question - what is this for?

I tripped over begging bowls in a line
Deliberated over a placard -
Carefully avoided residue slime
We can never look too hard

Our grandfathers thought dirt would disperse
Through technology's advance
But desperate greedy need can't be wrong
When we have trains right through to France

If you need a slave, they are there for the plucking
Look for a skull with no eyes
I think I hear a booted leg kicking
Perhaps anger's alive in those cries

Peanut-Crunching At Plath's Table

Of the peanut crunchers, I am one.
I have a heart-plush red seat, first row.
I squint, take out binoculars, adjust them,
again and again.

Of the muck-mud slingers, I am blackened
from poking the ashes of the bonfire of your life.
I wipe soot from my fingers onto my brazen
burning cheek.

Of the poetic sludge-sluts, I am the slipshod
slapper. Cross-referencing the photos, the
tattered tittle-tattle. Grabbing gossip as I
shamefully submerge into your psyche.

Of the Godless Goddesses, you are the one.
The literary Marilyn, acting out our nightmares
of betrayals; a panicked butterfly
between two mugs of milk.

Of the eternally prurient, we have all become one,
shuffling our assumptions, like your pack of cards.
We are dazzled, dreamy, from the soap-opera
suicide that jellies our eyes.

The necropolis is silent, save for the sound of the gasp-gaping shells,
mouthing a crack under my shoes.

I sieve through the debris that the popcorn professors
have shed. I salvage luminescent kernels, melt soft and sad on my tongue.

They provide me with the protein to cry.
I proffer this, my only sacrifice.
A saline apology.

Peter - In Memoriam

Sky-tinted goggles, sun-bed king,
the rays often warmed you, but
sometimes the UV lights were frost-blue
and you felt the chill.

I saw azure in your eyes and hoped
the ice would melt -
it cracked, drifted, so all would be clear,
for a week, a month...

I still feel you parted frothy oceans, but
couldn't see the sea-bed for waves -

If only you'd glanced behind,
you might have seen bronze-yellow
pebbles, nectarine sunsets -

but scratch the surface,
you were always gold.

Posthumous Prose

It's all right, you can step over me
It's not worth you checking my pulse
It fluttered and ebbed some time ago
Don't bother to call an ambulance

There can be no resuscitation
The cardiac monitor will only register
A straight line
No hopeful zig-zag graph of life for me

My skin took on the blue-ish pallor
Now I think rigor-mortis has set in
If you see me lying beneath your feet
Check my pockets, find this piece of paper

Send it to whom it may, or may not, concern
This is my posthumous prose

Species Under Threat

Why don't you send a letter-bomb
to those who have made me writhe
in unspeakable torment?
The bosses, the doctors, my father -
I don't see any demonstrations
outside my front door, my cage,
or anyone collecting petitions
to free me from captivity.
I prowl in invisible leg-irons,
my allotted space leaves me no room to breathe.
Occasionally, gawpers throw cigarettes
through bars - I snatch at them feverishly.
Is this humane? This must violate some law
of nature. No-one speaks out as I roar.
Soon I will be extinct.

The Missing Generation

Echoes of guns stuttered near, eggs laid, plans.
There was so much to do. The timer
cast a shadowy proclamation. Yolk yellow sand.
Full and gritty. The pity of war.

Husband as Captain, Fatherland in your smile,
nursing an optimistic, tiny platoon. All so raw.
But I couldn't fathom the incessant scarlet streams.
Was I mortally wounded?

All the babies never brought to fruition, gurgles stifled;
the birth of death, crosses upon crosses.

The land tried one final blast before zero hour.
Some watched the battle from a higher ground,
their hearts full of dread.
Down to timing again.
The wheels of war.
Dawn, dusk, set in stone.

The shock of the shell-hole at Boissellle, deeper, more
empty than death. There were so many battalions.
There were none. It was over. Was it never to be over?

Eventually, the deluge lessened. Dribbled sporadically into
still damaged psyches. Severed limbs are given prosthetics.
Surgeons stitched some sense of days unlived onto
charred faces. It is said some things can virtually be re-grown.

Still. The pounding has ceased.

Your eyes are life itself; hold me and we will say
a prayer for all the dead boys
and all the children
that never were.

To Dust

A cat is miaowing somewhere in my head;
barbed wire held tight around my neck
by some unseen, obscene force that
tries to asphyxiate me when I breathe.
A million demon goblins dance around my heart,
cackling cockroaches run gleefully along every nerve,
pickled piranhas nibble steadily at my flesh.
With each step, each inhalation of air,
I am disintegrating: I no longer know my name,
my blankness is mirrored in loved ones' eyes;
I have ceased to exist.

Xmas '93

The day came, complete with sooty darkness
like any other.

Pulling on grey with coal-blackened holes
the same as yesterday.

The mirror turned sulkily, held no attraction
just like tomorrow.

The presents crackled, ice-cream cold and their
origin eluded me.

Skittery voices uncoiled, unheeding, as the leaden lift
clanked me downstairs.

The fire, festooned with pine-cones sprayed in gold
was devoid of any warmth.

Mulled wine leaked, limping, and on my tongue
rolled bitter black stains.

Amber anger illuminated my face, lit blue pink and green
as fairy-tree lights winked and patronised.

Yuletide spun, as ivy-green mist thickly obliterated
all hopes of a Christmas truce.

Some Velvet Morning

Not one of us knew the time,
none of us cared.
We only knew it was late -
but it wouldn't end for a good while yet.

We were where everyone wanted to be
at that time, in THE club where
anything could happen - and did.
The whole of the country envied us
for being at the centre of this seamy,
gothic world of light and dark, love and hate,
sex interlaced with sadism.
Excess was lauded as an art form.

A record came on, maybe around 4.00am:
'Some Velvet Morning', the singer intoned.
We looked at each other, listened.
It had captured our mood so accurately.
After it ended, we all said we would not
forget this night. It was one of those
sunlit, spider-web moments that cannot be
swept away.

Where will we all be in 20 years? we asked
each other, laughing at the possible scenarios.
Luckily, the ghosts of our futures were not there
amongst us that night to heap scorn upon us.

Shelly, with her alluring cat's eyes and
Debbie Harry lips, married a soldier and contracted
a virulent strain of ME. She hasn't worked since.
Debs, with her heart-face and elfin looks, was
diagnosed with Multiple Sclerosis as she turned 30.
Beautiful, Boyish Cat went the way many junkies do.
She went on the streets and died a tragic, hooker's death.

And what of me - with my tight black dress,
peroxide hair and a body that had turned Men into
pitiful, pleading, puddles?

I suffered a long episode of clinical depression and wept as the
drugs they fed me bloated me and my features dissolved,
until I was unrecognisable.

Now? I am just waiting, hoping for another velvet morning

Danny Boyle, Darkness & The 27 Club

It's the first Saturday of the Olympics and the
pollen shoots into the heart of my immunity like
V2s yet it's odd how the more my nose pours
words snatches of lyrics ping-pong around my
crater-box-brain but who wants to watch table
-tennis when you can flinch at two Austrians
trying to anschluss their way through the Murray
brothers Andy is still fighting his opponents and
demons so hard it amazes me the will of instinct
so Kurt's here is he vomiting his deviant twisted
thoughts into the atmosphere where they coagulate
into something so beautiful only the scared
scarred can comprehend I curse my fucking so
-called creativity which robs me of any
normality shit Andy wears that dark look the I
will not tolerate sub-standard serves face that
prompts him to throw his racket across the court
you can tell he wants to target Jamie's thick
skull hold tight Andy beware of no love lost
thank God for Danny Boyle's images which spear
sporadically through the tennis I loved it when
the boy looked at Johnny brave to go underground
and not care what society wants except yes we do
need Attlee's NHS which we should be so proud of
don't you dare fuck with it you bastards
in a useless wavering coalition then a quick
snatch of London Calling but blink and Amy has
vanished again so back to Wimbledon and Jamie's
serve still doesn't stand up to the better
brother's scrutiny so I sing Jamie Jamie Jamie
you know I've been here before but he doesn't of
course it's Amy who knows what becomes before and
after it all Christ I've collapsed onto the bed
so exhausted with so many events taking place
simultaneously now I'm gazing at the ceiling like
Polly Harvey under ether the snot lashes down
my throat like lava it scalds so show me the way
to the next whisky bar because a different
Polly's back hurts she's just as bored as me but
that bit's bollocks I feel more of a nauseous
numbness yet my hands tingle with panic it's my

heart careering thumping around like a boxing
match when I try to disentangle myself from
strait-jacket sheets I'm feverish wet and am
losing my body heat the cassette plays poptones
whilst I write with that sick compulsion I only
stop to piss sneeze wheeze weigh myself drink
more coffee so jittery sick with adrenaline and
fear someone help I know I am losing control fast
sanity sifts sand-like through my fingers as
rapidly as Ian's shadow faded he never made it to
27 yet Amy may be drawn to him because she too
gave them what they wanted she let them use her
for their own ends but she has found someone else
who knows he's no good she launches a package
fastened with a heart-shaped hair-grip with
Kurt's name on when he peels back the layers he
finds warm milk and laxatives ah sweet erratic
Amy is just a lost little girl who can't keep
still though one flutter from huge bat-winged
eyes may be enough to re-ignite Jim's smouldering
embers into that bright burning fire he yearns
for but don't forget Jimi he'd wear Amy well he
knows this is a golden soul-girl yeah he did that
thing through his guitar he beckons to her
through a fluorescent purple haze so which bad
boy path does she choose when she knows damn well
that as she canters spindly legs teetering in
fuck-me pumps down her lane crazy tumbledown hair
flying it will be the wrong track love is always
a losing game she runs petrified she will be left
to wake up alone facing her black so on the floor
by her feet there still sits that infamous bottle
well today seems to be all loss and the lost
losers are probably cowards they don't deserve
medals maybe Sunday I can revive a bit of the
dead in me tomorrow tomorrow will never belong to
people like us will it?

The following people moistened my dry cracked brain with bits of inspiration in their own way (all apologies for misinterpretations, misquotes and typos); Andy and Jamie Murray, Kurt Cobain (RIP), Danny Boyle, Tony Parsons and Julie Burchill, The Clash, the late, great Labour leader Clement Attlee, Ian Curtis (RIP), Polly Harvey, Paul Weller, John Lydon, Jim Morrison (RIP), Jimi Hendrix (RIP), Muse, Jeff Buckley (RIP), the Cocteau Twins and the incredible, unique Amy Winehouse (RIP). Last but not least, this is also a tribute to my great Mum who is thankfully still alive and creating but is also nearly as bonkers as me.

Author's Profile

Julia was born on Tyneside, where her young parents had met when her Scottish father was a student at Durham University and her mother a budding artist.

Bright, but sickly, she came through an unstable childhood to gain a BA degree in Cultural Studies, which proved to be a perfect stepping stone to her first job with the feminist publishing house Virago. She then went on to work as a publicist for Penguin books.

After taking time out to travel in South-East Asia, she returned with a viral illness which triggered a mental breakdown. For the rest of her life, she struggled with health problems, yet still managed a long spell working as a Senior Press Officer at head office of Mind, the mental health charity based in London.

The end of her marriage led to inpatient psychiatric treatment, until her untimely death in 2016.

From a young age, Julia was a prolific writer and voracious reader and this volume is a unique expression of her passions and life experiences. She lives on through her words.

Acknowledgements

A big thank you to John Wilks at Cerasus for taking on this project and giving Julia's manuscript some shape.

Thanks also to Claudine Lazar at ABCtales, who first broached the idea of publication.

Finally, much love and thanks to my daughter Sarah, who has always been there for me and Julia, through all the tough times along the way. Her contribution to this project has been invaluable and I hope the dedication speaks for itself.

Coral Jane

Printed in Poland
by Amazon Fulfillment
Poland Sp. z o.o., Wrocław